D1475356

The U.S. Combat Aircraft Industry

1909-2000

Structure
Competition
Innovation

Mark Lorell

Prepared for the Office of the Secretary of Defense

RAND

NATIONAL DEFENSE RESEARCH INSTITUTE

Approved for public release; distribution unlimited

The research described in this report was sponsored by the Office of the Secretary of Defense (OSD). The research was conducted in RAND's National Defense Research Institute, a federally funded research and development center supported by the OSD, the Joint Staff, the unified commands, and the defense agencies under Contract DASW01-01-C-0004.

RAND is a nonprofit institution that helps improve policy and decisionmaking through research and analysis. RAND® is a registered trademark. RAND's publications do not necessarily reflect the opinions or policies of its research sponsors.

Cover design by Peter Soriano

© Copyright 2003 RAND

Published 2003 by RAND
1700 Main Street, P.O. Box 2138, Santa Monica, CA 90407-2138
1200 South Hayes Street, Arlington, VA 22202-5050
201 North Craig Street, Suite 202, Pittsburgh, PA 15213-1516
RAND URL: http://www.rand.org/
To order RAND documents or to obtain additional information, contact Distribution Services: Telephone: (310) 451-7002; Fax: (310) 451-6915; Email: order@rand.org

Congress has expressed concerns about three areas of the U.S. fixed-wing combat aircraft industry:[1]

- Retention of adequate competition in the design, engineering, production, sale, and support of military aircraft

- Continued innovation in the development and manufacture of military aircraft

- Actual and future capability of more than one aircraft company to design, engineer, produce, and support military aircraft.

This report provides a brief survey of industry structure, innovation, and competition in the U.S. fixed-wing combat aircraft industry from its earliest days to the present. It supports a much larger research effort examining the future of the U.S. military aircraft industrial base that responds to the above three congressional concerns.

The overall RAND research effort on the future viability of the combat aircraft industry has four basic research questions, or tasks:

- How is the industry different now from what it was in the past?

- What do the industry's competition and innovation pictures look like today?

---

[1]As noted in Appropriation Conference Committee, *FY02 Defense Appropriations Act Report,* Washington, D.C.: House Report 107-350, 19 December 2001, Section 8162.

- What courses of action does the Department of Defense (DoD) have to affect competition and innovation in the future?

- What policy options emerge from these courses of action?

This report aims at providing part of the answer to the first research question. It carefully examines what the industry looked like in the past and how it evolved over time, and it emphasizes particularly the nature of the competition among prime contractors/integrators and the history of innovation in fixed-wing combat aircraft. The research reported here includes "lessons learned" from past experience and suggestions for further research that may contribute to developing answers to the other three overarching research questions listed above. It draws heavily on prior published and unpublished research sponsored by the United States Air Force and conducted under the auspices of the Resource Management Program of RAND's Project AIR FORCE.

Answers to all four questions are sought in a companion volume:

John Birkler, Anthony G. Brower, Jeffrey A. Drezner, Gordon Lee, Mark Lorell, Giles Smith, Fred Timson, William P. G. Trimble, and Obaid Younossi, *Competition and Innovation in the U.S. Fixed-Wing Military Aircraft Industry*, Santa Monica, Calif: RAND, MR-1656-OSD, 2003.

This research was sponsored by the Office of the Secretary of Defense (OSD) and was overseen by the Office of the Deputy Under Secretary of Defense for Industrial Policy. This research was conducted within the Acquisition and Technology Policy Center of RAND's National Defense Research Institute (NDRI), a federally funded research and development center (FFRDC) sponsored by OSD, the Joint Staff, the unified commands, and the defense agencies. NDRI is located within RAND's National Security Research Division.

CONTENTS

FIGURES

A RAND research effort sponsored by the Office of the Secretary of Defense examined the future of the U.S. fixed-wing military aircraft industrial base. Its focus was the retention of competition and innovation in the military aircraft industrial base. The first major research task in that study involved a careful examination of the evolution of the industry structure over time, which emphasized an analysis of the role of competition and its links to innovation throughout the history of the industry. This report provides our findings and "lessons learned" from that part of the larger RAND research project.

The purpose of this survey was to identify issues relevant to the current policy debate on whether adequate levels of competition and innovation in fixed-wing combat aircraft development can be maintained over future decades. The debate has arisen from two recent developments: (1) the dramatic reduction in the number of credible combat aircraft prime contractors and lower-tier suppliers as a result of extensive mergers and acquisitions—consolidation—throughout the past decade and (2) the continued reduction in the number of anticipated new development and production programs for manned combat aircraft over the same period.[1] It is often explicitly or im-

---

[1] In the 1990s, the number of credible U.S. prime contractors for the development of fixed-wing combat aircraft declined from seven to two. (Some observers would not include Northrop Grumman as a third because, in 2000, in spite of its prominent role on the Lockheed-Martin Joint Strike Fighter [JSF] program, it did not enjoy the status of prime contractor on any major manned fixed-wing military or commercial aircraft program.) At the beginning of the new millennium, only one new manned combat aircraft program—the JSF—seemed likely to be funded in the foreseeable future.

plicitly assumed that high innovation in combat aircraft design is associated with large numbers of prime contractors (developers), because large numbers of prime contractors indicate a high degree of competition.

The fundamental goal of this report is to review the history of the U.S. aircraft industrial base to determine what insights, if any, can be gained regarding this assumption. This report does not pretend to provide definitive or comprehensive answers. We fully recognize the inherent limitations of a relatively brief top-level survey that draws heavily on published material and other existing research that was often conducted for other purposes.[2]   Therefore, our objective is modest: We aim at identifying issues and questions based on past historical experience that may be indicative of what type of conditions may need to hold in the future for maintaining the level of competition and its potential linkage to innovation, in the hopes that our findings may inform strategies developed for bettering future DoD competition and innovation. Perhaps more realistically, it may point the way to future high-leverage research on the interaction of competition and innovation in the military aerospace industry.

Our analysis aims at identifying periods of revolutionary innovation in combat aircraft development and examining the aviation/ aerospace industry structure and the role of competition during these periods. By *revolutionary innovation,* we mean technological advances that were integrated at key points in history in ways that led to a fundamental transformation and large advances in the performance capabilities of combat aircraft. Our goal is to ascertain the numbers and types of prime contractors, the nature of the competition among them, and the links among industry structure, competition, and innovation. The focus is on prime contractors and

---

Development and production of the JSF F-35 fighter was expected to be led by only one prime contractor—Lockheed-Martin—raising concerns that, in future decades, the Department of Defense (DoD) would have only one experienced prime contractor to turn to for new fixed-wing combat aircraft development.

[2]This overview draws heavily on prior published and unpublished research sponsored by the USAF and conducted under the auspices of the Resource Management Program of RAND's Project AIR FORCE.

integrators involved in the design and development of combat aircraft (fighter, fighter/attack, and bomber aircraft).[3]

We used several databases to examine all contractors, by aircraft specialization, which competed in the period 1909 through 2000.[4] Our survey of the data suggests that it is possible and reasonable to identify at least five distinct technology eras over the history of fixed-wing heavier-than-air combat aircraft, as shown in Table S.1: the

Table S.1

Five Principal U.S. Technology Eras and Their Innovation Periods for Fighters and Bombers (Airframe/Engine), 1909–2000

Years	Era	Innovation Periods	
		Technology Revolution	Technology Refinement
1909–1931	Biplane	1909–1916	1916–1931
1931–1945	Prop monoplane	1931–1940	1940–1945
1945–1953	Subsonic jet	1942–1947	1947–1953
1953–1981	Supersonic jet		
	Early super-sonic jet	1953–1962	1962–1972
	Agile super-sonic jet	1972–1974	1974–1981
1981–present	Stealth	1981–1990	1990–present

---

[3]Many of the most important improvements in combat aircraft performance have resulted from technological innovation in power plant development. We fully recognize the key role played in aeronautics by research and development (R&D) in engine technology. However, the history of competition and innovation in the aircraft engine industry is a proper subject for a separate study and is not attempted in this report. A brief overview of this subject is available in O. Younossi, M. Arena, R. Moore, M. Lorell, J. Mason, and J. Graser, *Military Jet Engine Acquisition: Technology Basics and Cost-Estimating Methodology*, Santa Monica, Calif.: RAND, MR-1596-AF, 2002.

[4]These databases are drawn from earlier published and unpublished RAND research sponsored mainly by the USAF and conducted under the auspices of RAND Project AIR FORCE. Some of these data are available in Mark A. Lorell and Hugh P. Levaux, *The Cutting Edge: A Half Century of U.S. Fighter R&D*, Santa Monica, Calif.: RAND, MR-939-AF, 1998.

biplane era (1909–1931), the propeller (prop) monoplane era (1931–1945), the subsonic-jet era (1945–1953), the supersonic-jet era (1953–1981), and the stealth era (1981–present). The supersonic-jet era includes two major sub-eras: the early supersonic-jet sub-era (1953–1972) and the agile supersonic-jet sub-era (1972–1981). Each of these eras began with a period of revolutionary innovation, high rates of technology advancement, and significant improvements in performance.

Each technology era and sub-era is divided into an initial period of revolutionary technological change and innovation ("technology revolution"), followed by a period of less-revolutionary technological change, characterized by refinement and consolidation of the technology advances first applied during the revolutionary period ("technology refinement").

Our broad assessment of the industry dynamics during each of the historical technology eras produced a variety of observations and hypotheses, most of which require further testing and analysis and further research to determine their validity and applicability to the current and future conditions that may characterize the U.S. combat aircraft industrial base. Providing a guide for further research,[5] they include the following:

- Each of the five historical technology eras began with distinct periods characterized by bursts of dramatically increased innovation in combat aircraft. The resulting new combat aircraft based on new designs and technology exhibited large advances in performance capabilities over the previous generation of combat aircraft.

- The initial periods of high technological innovation that began each technology era were all characterized by an increased competition to innovate among at least seven experienced, credible prime contractors/integrators specializing in combat aircraft.

- Following the initial period of increased innovation that started each new technology era, prime contractors tended to focus on

---

[5]RAND has conducted a larger parallel study of projected future conditions and structure of the defense aerospace industry to test these and other hypotheses. See Birkler et al., 2003.

refinement of the new technologies and configuration that had recently emerged. Except for the period of biplane technology consolidation in the 1920s, these periods were also characterized by vigorous competition among at least seven credible prime contractors. Contractors continued to innovate, except at a pace that was slower and less revolutionary. Eventually, however, the designs and technologies characteristic of the specific technology era reached a point of dramatically diminishing marginal returns in engine/platform performance.

- After an initial industry shake-out following the period of high technology innovation in each new technology era, new dominant industry leaders among prime contractors/integrators emerged in key specialty areas in combat aircraft. Other companies declined to positions that could be characterized as second-rank or niche players with respect to reputation, winning program competitions, and/or sector sales.

- From the historical evidence, the precise relationship between competition and increased innovation at the beginning of each new technology era is unclear. The competition to innovate during these periods was usually triggered by factors related to increased market demand, various technology developments, and military threat perceptions and system requirements.

   More specifically, the types of factors that historically seem to be linked to high-innovation bursts and the increased competition to innovate that began each new technology era include (1) industry perceptions of a potential or actual increase in market demand, (2) maturity and applicability of new component technologies, particularly when a new design and technology approach promised to offer high returns in desirable performance improvements, and/or (3) significant changes in government buyer performance and capability requirements.

- The prime contractors that tended to be the technology leaders and greatest innovators during the periods with initial bursts of intense competition to innovate that began each new technology era, were most often not among the industry leaders of the prior technology-refinement era. Rather, they were one of the following types of firms:

- — Second-rank or niche prime contractors
- — Leader firms expanding outside their existing area of specialization
- — New entrants to the industry.

- The historical evidence suggests, but does not prove, that an industrial structure that includes numerous prime contractors during periods of slower technological advance, some of which are dominant in sales and some of which are second rank, is conducive to encouraging the onset of periods of higher innovation when demand changes and market conditions are right. To displace the dominant market leaders, second-rank firms are willing to take greater technological and financial risks, thus setting off an intense competition to innovate among many qualified contractors seeking market expansion.

- Our more detailed review of the 1920s and the early 1930s seems to support, but does not prove, the contention that larger numbers of experienced, credible prime contractors are more likely than lower numbers of competitors to promote the greater competition to innovate that leads to new technology eras. Unlike any other historical period, the post–World War I biplane era was dominated by only two credible and experienced developers of fighters and one or two leading developers of bombers. U.S. innovation in military aircraft slowed dramatically, to the point of stagnation, during this period. This period was characterized by both the smallest number of dominant prime contractors in fixed-wing military aircraft and arguably the lowest level of sustained technological innovation of any comparable period in U.S. aviation history. However, the relative lack of innovation during this period was also strongly influenced by the fairly low demand and lack of market opportunities. Furthermore, the existence of relatively low entry barriers meant that, when demand increased, competition and innovation went up.

- The historical evidence suggests, but does not prove, that higher levels of demand promote new entrants and much greater competition among contractors to innovate. The existence of only one or two dominant credible contractors, combined with high barriers to entry, may reduce the incentives for competition to innovate, even during periods of rising demand.

These findings raise potentially serious questions about the level of competition and innovation in a future environment that may be dominated by only one or two prime contractors with the credible capability to develop a new-generation fixed-wing combat aircraft. These questions require further study and analysis.

ACRONYMS

AF	Air Force
ATA	Advanced Tactical Aircraft
ATB	Advanced Technology Bomber
ATF	Advanced Tactical Fighter
BA	Budget Authority
BAE	British Aerospace
CAD	computer-assisted design
CAIV	Cost As an Independent Variable
CAS	close air support
CDRR	Concept Development and Risk Reduction
CIA	Central Intelligence Agency
CFC	carbon-fiber composite
COIN	counterinsurgency
CSIRS	Covert Survivable In-weather Reconnaissance/ Strike
CY	calendar year
DARPA	Defense Advanced Research Projects Agency

Dem/Val	demonstration and validation
DoD	Department of Defense
FBW	fly-by-wire
FFRDC	federally funded research and development center
FY	fiscal year
GD	General Dynamics
GEC	General Electric Company
HALE UAV	high-altitude long-endurance unmanned air vehicle
JSF	Joint Strike Fighter
JSTARS	Joint Surveillance Target Attack Radar System
LANTIRN	Low-Altitude Navigation and Targeting Infrared System for Night
LO	low observable
LPI	low probability of intercept
LTV	Ling-Temco-Vought
LWF	Lowe, Willard and Fowler Engineering Company
NACA	National Advisory Committee for Aeronautics
NASA	National Aeronautics and Space Administration
NDRI	National Defense Research Institute
OSD	Office of the Secretary of Defense
R&D	research and development
RAM	radar-absorbing material
RCS	radar cross section
RDT&E	Research, Development, Test and Evaluation

RFI	Request for Information
RFP	Request for Proposal
TY	then year
UAV	Unmanned Air Vehicle
UCAV	Unmanned Combat Air Vehicle
UK	United Kingdom
USAAC	United States Army Air Corps
USAAF	United States Army Air Force
USAAS	United States Army Air Service
USAF	United States Air Force
VTOL	Vertical Take Off and Landing
XST	Experimental Survivable Test Bed

Chapter One

INTRODUCTION

Recent RAND research (for example, Lorell and Levaux, 1998) suggests that a close historical relationship may exist between robust competition in the U.S. fixed-wing combat aircraft industry and technological innovation. This report provides a broad-brush, high-level overview of the history of competition and innovation in the U.S. fighter aircraft industrial base from selected periods from 1909, before World War I, to 2000.

The purpose of this survey is to identify issues relevant to the current policy debate over maintaining adequate levels of competition and innovation in fixed-wing combat aircraft development over future decades. These issues have arisen from two recent developments: (1) the dramatic reduction in the number of credible combat aircraft prime contractors and lower-tier suppliers as a result of extensive mergers and acquisitions (i.e., consolidation) throughout the past decade, and (2) the continued reduction in the number of anticipated new development and production programs for manned combat aircraft over the same period.[1] It is often explicitly or implicitly

---

[1]In the 1990s the number of credible U.S. prime contractors for the development of fixed-wing combat aircraft declined from seven to two. (Some observers would not include Northrop Grumman to make three, because in 2000, in spite of its prominent role on the Lockheed Martin Joint Strike Fighter [JSF] program, Northrop Grumman did not enjoy the status of prime contractor on any major manned fixed-wing military or commercial aircraft program.) At the beginning of the new millennium, only one new manned combat aircraft program—JSF—seemed likely to be funded in the foreseeable future. Development and production of the JSF F-35 fighter was expected to be led by only one prime contractor—Lockheed Martin—raising concerns that in future decades the Department of Defense (DoD) would have only one experienced prime contractor to turn to for new fixed-wing combat aircraft development.

assumed that high innovation in combat aircraft design is associated with large numbers of prime contractors (developers), where large numbers of prime contractors indicate a high degree of competition.[2] The fundamental goal of this report is to review the history of the U.S. aircraft industrial base to determine what insights, if any, can be gained regarding this assumption.

RESEARCH APPROACH AND KEY ISSUES

This report aims at identifying issues and questions, based on past historical experience, that may be indicative of what type of conditions may need to hold in the future regarding the level of competition and its potential linkage to innovation. Such information may better inform the formulation of future Department of Defense (DoD) competition and innovation strategies. Perhaps more realistically, it may point the way to future high-leverage research on the interaction of competition and innovation in the military aerospace industry. The report does not pretend to provide definitive or comprehensive answers. We fully recognize the inherent limitations of a brief top-level survey that draws heavily on published material and other existing research often conducted for other purposes.[3] Therefore, our objective is modest.

From our initial review of the historical data, we developed several questions on which to focus throughout this report:

1. Throughout the history of fixed-wing combat aircraft, is it possible to distinguish cycles of relatively rapid technological advance (or greater innovation) and contrast them with periods of relatively slower technological advance (less innovation) or of relative technological stagnation?

2. If so, what was the supply side of the equation for each period or cycle? That is, what was the structure of the industry, and the

---

[2]For a background discussion of competition and acquisition in relation to fighter aircraft, refer to Birkler et al. (2001).

[3]This overview draws heavily on prior published and unpublished research sponsored by the United States Air Force (USAF) and conducted under the auspices of the Resource Management Program of RAND Project AIR FORCE.

level and type of competition among prime contractors, during each period?

3. Likewise, what was the demand side of the equation? That is, what was the situation regarding commercial demand, U.S. government development and procurement of military aircraft, and foreign sales?

4. Is there any discernible pattern of progression over time regarding industry structure and leadership during cycles of rapid technology innovation and cycles of slower technology innovation or technology refinement?

5. If there is a pattern of progression, what apparent links exist among industry structure, market demand, competition, and levels of technological innovation for each type of period? Most important, what factors related to industry structure and competition appear to be crucial for promoting levels of greater technological innovation? Is there some critical minimum number of firms below which the rate of innovation appears to decline?

6. What factors trigger the transition from a period of slower technological advance or stagnation to a period of rapid technological advance? Are there any patterns to what types of companies in what type of environment take a leadership role in launching new periods of greater innovation?

7. To what extent do other factors, such as government support for basic aeronautical research, overall industry size, level and complexity of the underlying aircraft-system technology, the extent of overlap between commercial and military technologies, the government regulatory and contracting environment, and so forth, appear to affect the interplay of competition and innovation, and render clear-cut conclusions difficult?

Our initial survey of the evidence suggests that, in view of our limitations in data and resources, it is possible in some cases to provide only partial answers to these questions; in other cases, no definitive answers are possible at all. In addition, the answers to many of these questions appear to be far more complex and conditional than originally anticipated. Nonetheless, these questions are useful for providing guidance for our inquiry and in identifying areas in which further research will be beneficial.

TECHNOLOGY ERAS IN FIXED-WING COMBAT AIRCRAFT

Our focus is on prime contractors and integrators involved in the design and development of combat aircraft (fighter, fighter/attack, and bomber aircraft). Our survey of the data for this type of aircraft suggests that it is possible and reasonable to identify at least five distinct technology eras over the history of fixed-wing heavier-than-air aircraft (see Table 1.1): the biplane era (1909–1931), the propeller (prop) monoplane era (1931–1945), the subsonic-jet era (1945–1953), the supersonic-jet era (1953–1981), and the stealth era (1981–present). The supersonic-jet era includes two major sub-eras: the early supersonic sub-era (1953–1972) and the agile supersonic jet sub-era (1972–1981). Each technology era and sub-era is divided into an initial period of revolutionary technological change and innovation ("technology revolution"), followed by a period of less-revolutionary technological change, characterized by refinement and consolidation of the technology advances first applied during the revolutionary period ("technology refinement").

This distinction is necessary because each of these eras began with a period of revolutionary innovation, high rates of technology advancement, and significant improvements in performance. By *revolutionary innovation,* we mean technological advances that were integrated together in new ways, leading to a fundamental transformation in the basic standard configuration of combat-aircraft weapon systems and to large advances in the performance capabilities of combat aircraft. This period for each technology era was followed by a second period of less-radical technology innovation during which prime contractors refined and improved the new technology paradigm. Innovation and performance improvements—sometimes significant ones—continued during these periods of refinement and consolidation. However, the dominant design and technology paradigm tended to suffer from the problem of increasingly small marginal returns in desired performance improvements.

We selected these specific technology eras, and dates associated with them, on the basis of informed individual judgment. Alternative periods and dates are plausible. However, the periods we identify capture the most-significant and most-revolutionary eras of high-

Table 1.1

Five Principal U.S. Technology Eras and Their Innovation Periods for Fighters and Bombers (Airframe/Engine), 1909–2000

Years	Era	Innovation Periods	
		Technology Revolution	Technology Refinement
1909–1931	Biplane	1909–1916	1916–1931
1931–1945	Prop monoplane	1931–1940	1940–1945
1945–1953	Subsonic jet	1942–1947	1947–1953
1953–1981	Supersonic jet		
	Early super-sonic jet	1953–1962	1962–1972
	Agile super-sonic jet	1972–1974	1974–1981
1981–present	Stealth	1981–1990	1990–present

level technology innovation in *combat-aircraft weapon system platforms*, which include the basic airframe, engine, and flight avionics.[4] Such a characterization excludes many important associated areas, such as munitions, sensors, communications, and support. However, most informed observers would not dispute the legitimacy of the high-level airframe/engine technology categories that we have selected. The changes in technology, configuration, and capabilities represented by each era are widely and routinely recognized as revolutionary in the public literature.

Division of each era into an initial period of revolutionary change followed by a period of technology and refinement can obviously be challenged. Some would argue that, especially in the supersonic-jet era, combat aircraft have become so complex and involve such an

---

[4]Many of the most important improvements in combat aircraft performance have resulted from technological innovation in power-plant development. We fully recognize the key role played in aeronautics by R&D in engine technology. However, the history of competition and innovation in the aircraft engine industry is a proper subject for a separate study and is not attempted in this report. A brief overview of this subject is available in O. Younossi, M. Arena, R. Moore, M. Lorell, J. Mason, and J. Glaser, *Military Jet Engine Acquisition: Technology Basics and Cost-Estimating Methodology*, Santa Monica, Calif.: RAND, MR-1596-AF, 2002.

enormous array of technologies, that high levels of innovation in one area or another have been virtually constant. However, we would still maintain that, when consideration is limited to the basic airframe/engine configuration and technology, our high-level characterization is essentially valid.

The dates we selected to bound our technology eras and innovation periods within eras are not in any sense claimed to be authoritative or absolute, but rather are meant to be a guide for the reader. Clearly, some overlap exists between periods, as we have recognized in our categorization. Indeed, in his characterization of fighter-aircraft generations during the jet era, a leading authority such as Richard Hallion (1990) has selected periods with significant and sometimes nearly total overlap.[5] This seems acceptable, since his findings, as well as ours, do not appear to be intrinsically dependent on precise adherence to the exact dates for eras and phases.

In most instances, the dates we chose represent symbolic events or years. The initial date of each technology era is usually, but not always, the first flight of the combat aircraft type that is generally recognized in the open literature as the pioneering combat aircraft for any given technology era. To qualify, the aircraft had to have been a prototype intended from design inception for development as an operational combat aircraft: It could not be a pure test vehicle or a technology demonstrator such as an "X" aircraft. The beginning of the technology-refinement period of a technology era is usually dated either from the first flight of the most-prominent "flagship" combat aircraft type that is widely recognized in the literature as the most successful or most prominent type of production combat aircraft of that technology era, or from the year that the services generally accepted the new technology and configuration as the baseline for all new fighters and bombers.[6]

---

[5]Richard Hallion (1990, pp. 4–23), a leading Air Force authority on the history of jet fighters, divides jet-fighter development into six generations: high subsonic (1943–1950), transonic (1947–1955), early supersonic (1953–1960), supersonic, limited purpose (1955–1970), supersonic, multi-role (1958–1980), and supersonic multi-role, high efficiency (1974–present). These generations are more detailed and refined than our high-level eras, and they do not necessarily conflict with our categorization. Also note that Hallion's generations entail considerable overlap in time.

[6]The rationale for the dates selected is as follows. 1909 is the year in which the Aeronautical Division of the Office of the Chief Signal Officer of the U.S. Army ac-

NUMBERS OF COMPETING PRIME CONTRACTORS

One logical and elementary first step in investigating possible links between the level of competition among prime contractors and the degree of innovation taking place is to flesh out the supply side by identifying the number of credible experienced prime contractors at any given time that were potential competitors for any given type of development contract for fixed-wing combat aircraft.

In the late 1990s, RAND developed two extensive databases that have been used to support analysis of the relationship of prime contractor experience and success at winning competitions and following through on development programs. The first database includes basic program information on all jet-fighter aircraft and fighter-like prototypes developed by U.S. industry since the beginning of the jet era in the early 1940s.[7] The second database includes most U.S. contractors that developed and produced fixed-wing and rotary-wing aircraft between 1910 and 2000, and emphasizes fighter and fighter/attack aircraft. The type of aircraft the contractor specialized in is also identified. The contractors are grouped in 5-year incre-

---

cepted the first military aircraft (a Wright Model B). 1916 is the generally accepted year during which the standard biplane fighter configuration became firmly established. 1931 was the first flight of the Boeing B-9 bomber, universally recognized as the first example of the modern monoplane combat aircraft. The most famous prop fighter ever developed, the North American P-51, first flew in October 1940. The P-51 is symbolic of the pinnacle of the monoplane fighter technology revolution. The Bell P-59, the first U.S. operational jet fighter, initially flew in 1942. In 1947, the North American F-86 fighter first flew. This aircraft established the predominance of the standard swept-wing jet-fighter configuration and went on to become the most famous of the subsonic-jet fighters. The first operational supersonic-jet fighter, the North American F-100, flew initially in 1953. 1962 witnessed the first flight of the ultimate supersonic bomber, the North American B-70. The McDonnell-Douglas F-15, the pioneer aircraft of the new generation of highly agile supersonic fighters, first flew in 1972. In 1974, the two flagship fighters of this technology era first flew: the YF-16 and the YF-17 (later F-16 and F-18). 1981 saw the maiden flight of the first operational stealth fighter, the Lockheed F-117. The Lockheed YF-22 and the Northrop YF-23, the prototypes of the competitors for the future standard Air Force Advanced Tactical Fighter supersonic stealth fighter, first flew in 1990.

[7]This database includes crucial milestone dates and contractor information on all major variants of all U.S. production jet fighters and jet fighter/attack aircraft for all the services, as well as all jet or rocket-powered fighter-like experimental aircraft and other types of test aircraft, and numerous fighter-like unmanned aerial vehicles (UAVs) and cruise missiles. In addition, it includes most large fixed-wing commercial jet passenger transport aircraft. For an overview and explanation of the database, see Lorell and Levaux (1998).

ments for purpose of analysis.[8] An overview of the number of significant U.S. contractors, by specialization, derived from these databases is shown in Figure 1.1. This figure shows that the number of major prime contractors shot up from about three in 1910 to almost 30 in 1935, then stabilized at about 25 by 1940 and remained at this number through the early 1960s. In the 1960s, the industry experienced a consolidation, with the number of primes declining from about 25 to just over 20. Beginning in the late 1980s, a new period of much more dramatic consolidation is evident. By 2000, the number of major prime contractors had declined by nearly 50 percent, from 20 to 11.

Figure 1.2 shows the same data but includes only contractors that specialized in fixed-wing combat aircraft (fighters, fighter/attack aircraft, and bombers). The same trends are evident. However, some important distinctions can be made. The data show that no U.S. prime contractors specialized in combat aircraft in 1915. Throughout most of the 1920s, only five contractors showed this specialization. In the early 1930s, a dramatic increase in the number of firms is indicated, peaking at around 16 in 1945. Thus, as a result of the economic mobilization of World War II, prime contractors with areas of combat aircraft specialization expanded to the largest number in history. The end of the war witnessed mass cancellations of huge planned production programs, spurring a sharp and rapid decline in prime contractors with military aircraft specializations, from 16 down to 11 by the mid-1950s. This number remained constant for about a decade, then declined to eight from the mid-1960s to the mid-1970s.

---

[8]This second database was developed by the author. It is an unpublished, internal RAND research resource. The designation of specialization by aircraft type is based on informed judgment. It derives from an examination of the types of aircraft the contractor typically developed and most successfully marketed. The industry-specialization categories are Air Force fighters, Navy fighters, Air Force and Navy fighters, fighters and bombers, bombers, other military fixed wing, helicopters, and commercial/other.

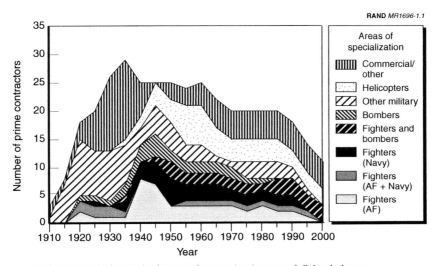

NOTE: In addition to the larger prime contractors specializing in larger commercial and military fixed-wing aircraft, this figure includes most of the smaller leading commercial prime contractors specializing in general-aviation aircraft, business aircraft, and rotary-wing aircraft

Figure 1.1—Major U.S. Prime Contractors by Aircraft Specialization, 1910–2000

Seven to eight combat aircraft primes remained active until the end of the Cold War.[9] In the decade of the 1990s, the industry experienced a period of dramatic consolidation—much more radical than that following World War II—as it retrenched in the face of declining procurement budgets. By the beginning of the new millennium, at best only three military aircraft primes remained: Lockheed-Martin, Boeing, and Northrop Grumman.[10]

---

[9]There are eight if LTV (formerly Ling-Temco-Vought) is treated as a potential prime contractor; there are seven if it is not.

[10]Some observers would not include Northrop Grumman in this list because, in 2000, in spite of its prominent role on the Lockheed-Martin JSF program, it did not enjoy the status of prime contractor on any major manned fixed-wing military or commercial aircraft program.

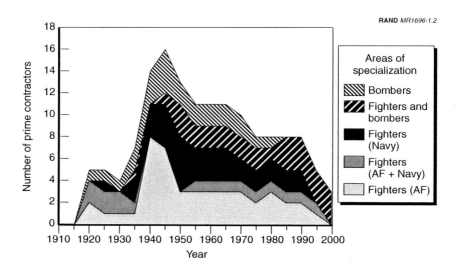

**Figure 1.2—Major U.S. Prime Contractors with Areas of Combat Aircraft
Specialization (Bombers and Fighters)**

What was the competitive structure of the aerospace industry in
numbers of firms with aircraft specializations during the key technology eras that we have already identified? Figure 1.3 overlays the
principal technology eras for combat aircraft on the total numbers of
military aircraft prime contractors by specialization for any given
time period, as shown in Figure 1.2. The most striking observation to
emerge from this simple exercise is that, with the exception of the
technology refinement and consolidation period of the biplane era,
all eras are characterized by at least seven to eight major combat-
aircraft prime contractors/integrators, many of whom specialized in
specific types of combat aircraft.

Beyond these basic observations, this simple exercise is not very revealing. On the surface, it appears that plenty of potential for significant competition existed in all eras, during both the innovation
periods and the refinement periods, with the possible exception of
the 1920s and early 1930s. Historically, far more prime-contractor

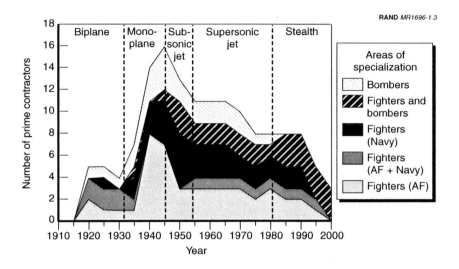

**Figure 1.3—Prime Contractors During the Five Principal Air
Vehicle/Engine Combat-Aircraft Technology Eras**

competitors have existed during all five of our technology eras, during both the revolutionary-innovation periods and the refinement periods, than exist now. To gain additional insight into the possible links between competition and innovation, we must examine the eras in greater depth, particularly with respect to the demand side of the equation and the many other factors listed at the beginning of this chapter.

Nonetheless, Figure 1.3 points to the interesting possibility that the period of the 1920s and early 1930s might be particularly revealing, since that is the only historical period in which very few prime contractors dominated the development and production of fixed-wing military combat aircraft. In addition, it is a far less well-known and well-documented period in U.S. military aviation development and procurement history. For these reasons, the next two chapters focus on this early period. The jet periods are reviewed in Chapters Four and Five, and the stealth era is reviewed in Chapter Six, but on a more general level. For the most part, Chapters Four through Six are drawn directly from previously published RAND research on the relationship between contractor experience and contractor success in fixed-wing combat aircraft (Lorell and Levaux, 1998; Lorell, 1996)

Chapter Two

INDUSTRY STRUCTURE AND COMPETITION IN THE BIPLANE ERA

The United States, with such aviation pioneers as Orville and Wilbur Wright and Glenn H. Curtiss, led the world in innovation in heavier-than-air aircraft at the beginning of the twentieth century. During much of the first decade of aviation history, the aircraft industry remained a highly competitive but tiny specialized cottage industry that designed and produced small numbers of handcrafted airplanes in small workshops for wealthy enthusiasts (Vander Meulen, 1991).[1]

From 1903 to 1914, aviation pioneers in the United States and Europe proved to be extremely innovative and produced spectacular advances in performance capabilities. In December 1903, the Wright Flyer's first three flights were all under one minute and covered less than a thousand feet. By 1914, some aircraft had unrefueled ranges of over 600 miles (mi), top speeds of nearly 130 miles per hour (mph), and ceilings of more than 20,000 feet (ft).

As we shall see, such performance was not dramatically less than that of the frontline biplane fighters of the late 1920s and early 1930s. However, it is difficult to draw lessons from this period for the modern era. In some respects, this period in aviation history was comparable to the early stages of the personal-computer revolution of the

---

[1]Jacob A. Vander Meulen's *The Politics of Aircraft: Building an American Military Industry*, Lawrence, Kansas: University Press of Kansas, 1991, is a detailed but somewhat eccentric scholarly work on the structure and economics of the early U.S. military aircraft industry through the beginning of World War II. Vander Meulen focuses on government regulation of the industry, contracting, and procurement approaches, at the expense of technology innovation and development.

1970s and early 1980s, when individual entrepreneurs on shoestring budgets worked out of their garages developing revolutionary technologies and concepts that would later result in the Information Revolution.

U.S. INDUSTRY FALLS BEHIND IN WORLD WAR I

Of more relevance for us is how these performance innovations and developments were transferred to new weapon systems and industrialized on a large scale in the military procurement systems of large modern states.

This transition did not take place until World War I, when the vast increases in weapons-procurement spending necessitated by the demands of global warfare led to unprecedented economic mobilization of entire national economies and technology infrastructures. The late U.S. entry into the war meant that the U.S. aircraft industry had much less time to respond to high procurement budgets and the high demand for technological innovations to meet the new requirements of total war. Indeed, well before the United States entered the war, U.S. industry had already begun losing its technological leadership position in heavier-than-air military aircraft. This loss was due in part to a contentious litigation battle over patent rights between the Wright brothers and Glenn L. Curtiss, three of the foremost American aviation pioneers and innovators before the war, as well as to other factors (Vander Meulen, 1991).

Consequently, well before the outbreak of war in Europe, several European countries began moving ahead of the United States in leading-edge military aircraft technology developments. Soon, French pioneers pulled out in front of the pack, led by an impressive array of innovators, including Alberto Santos-Dumont, Léon Levavasseur, Gabriel and Charles Voisin, Henri Farman, Ambroise Goupy, Louis Blériot, Robert Esnault-Pelterie, Louis Breguet, Édouard de Niéuport, and Louis Béchereau. The French army, more than any other service, quickly recognized the military potential of aircraft. By 1912, it had increased its military aircraft inventory to over 250 planes. While the British and German armies lagged behind the French in this area, they too were more advanced than the U.S. Army (Prendergast, 1981).

The Aeronautical Division of the U.S. Army Signal Corps received its first military aircraft, a Wright Model B, only in mid-1909. It remained the Army's sole military aircraft for two years (Swanborough, 1963). American industry expanded output in response to gathering war clouds in Europe, but remained modest in size. The value of U.S. aircraft exports doubled from 1912 to 1914. Nonetheless, in 1914, the industry produced only 15 total aircraft for the domestic market while exporting another 34 (Bilstein, 2001).

The widening European lead in combat-aircraft configuration, technology, and operational doctrine vastly increased under the pressures of all-out war commencing on the Continent in August 1914. During the early months of World War I, militarized aircraft were used primarily for aerial observation of enemy land forces and dispositions, a mission comparable to the modern tactical fighter's reconnaissance role. The European belligerent powers experimented with a wide variety of airframe and engine configurations, but most early military aircraft had tandem seats accommodating a pilot and an observer. However, as the war progressed, the major belligerents soon developed the first true combat aircraft (both fighters and bombers) and the R&D and industrial infrastructures to support them. Innovation continued at a blistering pace during the war as the European combatants continuously struggled to gain and regain air superiority over the battlefield through the development of higher-performance, more-lethal fighter, attack, and bomber aircraft. Meanwhile, neutral America, briefly the world's leader in the development of heavier-than-air aircraft during the first decade of the century, lagged increasingly behind the Europeans as the war dragged on.

By 1916, the Europeans had settled on a basic fighter configuration, which remained dominant throughout the remainder of the war and well beyond. This configuration included a biplane layout, an open cockpit, fixed landing gear, a single forward-mounted, air-cooled radial engine or in-line water-cooled engine, and two forward-mounted machine guns synchronized to fire through the propeller arc. The fuselage was built of wood or, later, welded tubes, as were the wings, and covered with treated fabric or wood. Most heavy bombers were similar, but were most often equipped with two engines mounted between the wings outboard from the fuselage. Bombers often carried several gunners in open cockpits, armed with machine guns mounted on swivels. This basic configuration for both fighters and bombers predominated throughout the 1920s and well into the 1930s.

When the United States entered the war in April 1917, it had developed no mass-produced modern, indigenously developed fighter or bomber aircraft. U.S. aircraft companies had expanded significantly to meet the European war demand, but only two large companies predominated: Curtiss Aeroplane and Wright-Martin (Vander Meulen, 1991). During the war, almost all combat aircraft employed by the United States air service (organized within the U.S. Army Signal Corps) were of French or British design. Perhaps the most famous aircraft flown in support of the American Expeditionary Force in Europe was the French SPAD S.XIII used by American top ace Eddie Rickenbacker in the famous "Hat-in-a-Ring" 94th Aero Pursuit Squadron.[2,3]

During the war, the only indigenous design manufactured by U.S. industry in large numbers was the Curtiss JN-4 "Jenny," an unarmed training and utility aircraft.[4] With around 5,000 built during and immediately following the war, this simple two-seat aircraft was by far the most significant U.S. military aircraft of the era—a relatively modest achievement by European standards. For example, considerably more than 14,000 SPAD fighters were produced during the war. Production of the SPAD S.XIII variant alone, which began only in April 1917 when the United States entered the war, reached a total of 8,472 by the end of the war, with outstanding orders remaining for 10,000 more. Other well-known French fighters, such as the Niéuport series, were produced in large numbers. The other two most-capable fighters developed by the end of the war—the British Sopwith F.1 Camel and the German Fokker D.VII—had significant production runs but none nearly as large as those for the SPAD (Donald, 1999).

---

[2]SPAD is an acronym for *Société Pour l'Aviation et ses Dérivés* (Aircraft and Related Equipment Company), a company owned by Louis Blériot.

[3]The 94th Aero Pursuit Squadron was the first all-American fighter squadron to see combat (April 1918), and earned the highest number of enemy kills of any U.S. squadron (69 confirmed kills). See Auburn University Library's web site at http://www.lib.auburn.edu/archive/flyhy/101/eddie.htm#ww1.

[4]Glenn Curtiss founded the Curtiss Aeroplane Company in December 1910.

After U.S. entry into the war, planning began for large-scale domestic licensed production of foreign fighters, including the SPAD and the British Bristol F.2B. In August 1917, Congress passed the $640-million "Aero Bill,"[5] the largest congressional appropriations bill in U.S. history up to that point. However, severe problems were encountered in trying to implement the massive U.S. combat-aircraft production effort, because of the problems of rapidly transitioning a crafts-based cottage industry into a Detroit-like mass-production heavy industry. In the end, the wartime production program fell far short of expectations and was widely perceived as a failure and scandal (Bilstein, 2001; Vander Meulen, 1991; Pattillo, 2000).

Following the Armistice on 11 November 1918, the U.S. government decided against licensed production of foreign types in favor of development of indigenous designs. Following the formation of the separate U.S. Army Air Service in April 1918, officials developed plans for a postwar force structure of over 5,000 military aircraft. However, Congress drastically cut procurement funding in the wake of the Armistice. As a result, by mid-1924, the U.S. Army Air Service possessed only 78 pursuit (fighter) aircraft out of a total inventory of nearly 1,400 aircraft (Munson, 1970).

LOW DEMAND, LACK OF COMPETITION STIFLE INNOVATION

Reflecting the United States' return to isolationism with the rejection of the Versailles Treaty, defense budgets, force structures, and procurement remained low throughout the 1920s. The Europeans also cut back drastically after the war, but not nearly to the levels witnessed in the United States. At the end of the war, France boasted the largest and best-equipped air force in the world. Although France reduced its force structure significantly, it still retained around 20,000 military aircraft in its active inventory well into the 1920s.

---

[5]The Aero Bill was the largest congressional appropriation to date and was intended to fund the manufacture of 20,000 aircraft. The bill passed despite hostility to aviation from the General Staff.

The rapid decline in military demand had a devastating effect on the industry. In 1917, U.S. military aircraft production had jumped 400 percent, from the production total of just over 400 the preceding year to over 2,000 aircraft. In 1918, total military aircraft production exploded to over 14,000, then was slashed in 1919 to under 800 aircraft. By 1922, annual production had plummeted to 263. Investment in the aircraft industry in 1919–1920 declined by about 90 percent from the preceding year (Pattillo, 2000; Vander Meulen, 1991).

As Figure 2.1 shows, Army and Navy total air appropriations declined and remained low in the early and mid-1920s, rising slightly as the decade progressed. These slight increases failed to bring spending anywhere close to the levels attained during World War I, or even to the levels of the immediate postwar period. Figure 2.2 shows total U.S. aircraft production from 1917 through 1927. It shows two important points: the dramatic decline in overall production from the huge levels of the war years, and the total domination of military production until late in the 1920s decade. This shift toward greater commercial production would have important consequences, as discussed in the next chapter.

Another problem from the industry perspective was that, because the government owned the design data, it usually contracted separately on a price-competition basis for R&D and production. Thus, a design developed by one company, usually at considerable company expense, might be competed for production and could end up being produced by a competitor. Another approach commonly practiced by both the Army and Navy was to design new aircraft organically and build prototypes in-house, then outsource the production contracts to commercial companies. (For a detailed discussion of the severe burdens placed on industry by government policies regarding competition, contracting regulations, and intellectual-property rights, see Vander Meulen, 1991, and Bowers, 1989.)

Companies routinely lost money on military R&D contracts. Separately competed production contracts on a best-price basis encouraged companies to reduce their R&D and engineering staffs to a minimum in order to slash overhead costs and make them more competitive in bids for production contracts (Vander Meulen, 1991). Such policies for contracting and intellectual-property rights probably inhibited company R&D investment and innovation.

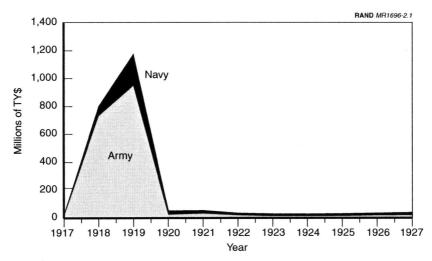

SOURCE: Data are from Donald M. Pattillo, *Pushing the Envelope: The American Aircraft Industry*, Ann Arbor, Michigan: The University of Michigan Press, 2000, Tables 1 and 3.
    NOTE: *Air appropriations* include other procurement and other expenditures in addition to the procurement of aircraft.

Figure 2.1—U.S. Army and Navy Air Appropriations, 1917–1927

In short, low procurement budgets and low demand, combined with contracting policies that industry considered onerous and a global market dominated by more technologically advanced foreign competitors, made the combat aircraft market unattractive to the U.S. aircraft industry in the 1920s. The U.S. services purchased specific types of military aircraft in very small numbers and small lot sizes, making more economical and potentially more profitable longer production runs impossible.

The commercial market could not make up for the lack of military orders. There *was* no viable commercial market. In the early and mid-1920s, the military market was the backbone of the industry, although it remained small and uncertain, as shown in Figure 2.2. After 1920, the U.S. government vigorously promoted and indirectly

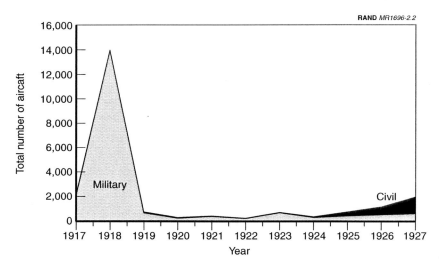

SOURCE: Data are from Donald M. Pattillo, *Pushing the Envelope: The American Aircraft Industry*, Ann Arbor, Michigan: The University of Michigan Press, 2000, Tables 2 and 4.

Figure 2.2—U.S. Military and Commercial Aircraft Production, 1917–1927

subsidized private airlines for transporting airmail—a small but relatively assured market for aircraft developers, and one that became an important focus for aircraft designers and manufacturers. However, this market was so small that it failed to spur the kind of large-scale investment necessary to promote the type of vigorous innovation that would produce revolutionary changes in design and performance. Although helping to keep the aviation industry alive, the subsidized airmail commercial sector failed to stimulate dramatic new innovations in overall platform configuration and performance (Heppenheimer, 1995). Consequently, the basic configuration, performance, and materials for fighters and bombers, which had become well established by 1916, remained predominant throughout the 1920s.

Under these circumstances, numerous prime contractors withdrew from the military market or the entire aircraft market. In the years immediately following the war, important military aircraft developers that exited the industry include Standard; Gallaudet; Thomas-Morse; Lowe, Willard and Fowler Engineering Company; Dayton-

Wright; and Aeromarine. The demise of Thomas-Morse, the designer of a reasonably successful indigenous fighter design (based on the French SPAD), can be directly traced to the award of the production contract to Boeing, which had little ability to design an advanced fighter but which underbid Morse on the production contract (see the following section, "U.S. Fighter Development During the Biplane Era"). Small companies, including such leading firms as Curtiss and Consolidated Aircraft, continued on, but experienced severe financial losses.

Given these circumstances, it is not surprising that, fairly rapidly, only two companies came to dominate the design, development, and production of all U.S. fighter aircraft throughout the 1920s and into the early 1930s: Boeing and Curtiss. During the same period, two other companies served the indigenous bomber market: Martin and Keystone.

From 1919 through 1925, the U.S. Army Air Service (USAAS) let contracts worth slightly over $20 million[6] to the top 23 U.S. Army aircraft contractors, both aircraft prime contractors and second-tier equipment and subsystem suppliers, as shown in Figure 2.3. Of this total, 35 percent went in roughly equal shares to the two leading fighter producers: Boeing and Curtiss. Only two other fighter developers were even close, Aeromarine and Thomas-Morse; both had total contract awards at about one-third of each of the shares of the two leaders. This second duo of contractors exited the industry soon after the war, owing to high financial losses. Several other companies had entered the fighter market but remained very small. Most performed poorly financially and soon withdrew (e.g., Gallaudet, Loening). Glenn L. Martin was the only other large prime contractor during this period, its total contract value about half that of Boeing and Curtiss. Martin dominated the bomber market totally in the first part of the 1920s; Huff-Daland, which later became Keystone, became an important player in this bomber market only later in the second half of the 1920s (see the section "U.S. Bomber Development During the Biplane Era" later in this chapter).

---

[6]Compare this total with the $640 million Aero Bill authorization of August 1917.

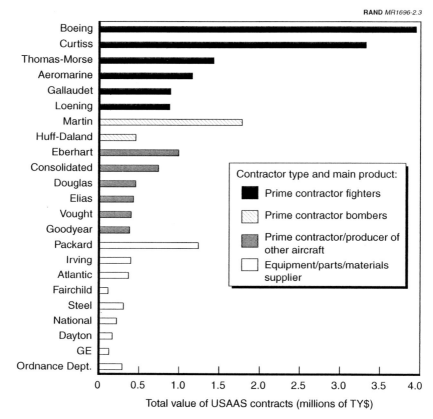

Figure 2.3—U.S. Army Air Service Top Contractors, 1919–1925

SOURCE: Based on data from the Office of the Chief of the Air Service, Procurement Section, Planning Branch Records, as presented in Jacob A. Vander Meulen, *The Politics of Aircraft: Building an American Military Industry*, Lawrence, Kansas: University of Kansas Press, 1991, Appendix 1.

Aircraft production-price contract data covering the years 1921 through 1927 for both the Army and the Navy, shown in Figure 2.4, indicate that Boeing and Curtiss not only monopolized all fighter production but also enjoyed significant bomber production (mostly

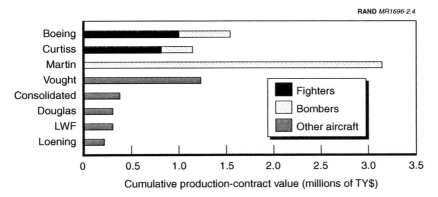

SOURCE: Based on data from the Office of the Chief of the Air Service, Procurement Section, Planning Branch Records, as presented in Jacob A. Vander Meulen, *The Politics of Aircraft: Building an American Military Industry*, Lawrence, Kansas: University of Kansas Press, 1991, Appendix 2.

Figure 2.4—Total Value (Quantity × Unit Price) of Major Army and Navy Aircraft Production Contracts by Contractor, 1921–1927

of other companies' designs).[7]   Martin, with the largest total production-contract value, clearly dominated bombers during this period.

Is there any direct evidence that this domination of the fighter market by two contractors and the bomber market by one or two contractors had any effect on innovation? Did the existence of only two or three dominant contractors reduce competition, thus suppressing innovation? What factors seemed to spur periods of greater innovation? We turn now to the more-detailed historical record to attempt to gain insight, if not definitive answers, into at least some aspects of these questions for the 1920s and the 1930s.

In the following two sections, we review the main U.S. fighter and bomber procurements during the first decade and a half following World War I, and show how three or four firms dominated the mar-

---

[7]As shown by data from United States Congress, *Hearings Before the Subcommittee on Aeronautics,* 73rd Congress, 1st Session, 1934, as listed in Vander Meulen (1991, Appendix Two).

ket. We also survey the combat aircraft technology developments of the period, arguing that little significant technology innovation occurred on combat aircraft that were procured by the services. We conclude by noting that a plausible circumstantial case can be made for linking the relative lack of competition during the period and the low level of innovation.

U.S. FIGHTER DEVELOPMENT DURING THE BIPLANE ERA

Curtiss

Curtiss, which developed Navy observation seaplanes and the famous Jenny training and utility aircraft during World War I, developed the first successful, fully indigenous U.S. fighter after the war. After the war, Curtiss remained one of the strongest U.S. aircraft companies financially and technologically.

The U.S. government subsidized aircraft manufacturers such as Curtiss to develop high-performance aircraft to enter into air races. In 1920, Curtiss began work on advanced high-performance fighter-like aircraft for racing in such events as the Pulitzer Trophy Race and the Schneider Trophy Race. The Army and the Navy often sponsored development of racing aircraft. These aircraft, often piloted in races by service members, benefited technologically from the intense racing rivalry between the two services (Bilstein, 2001).

Curtiss' dominant position during World War I and throughout the early postwar years permitted it to exploit the experience gained from racing planes to develop an indigenous fighter that would maintain its dominant position in the U.S. military aircraft market. In 1922, Curtiss used company funds to develop its own unique fighter design, the PW-8, for both the Navy and Army. That design was based on experience gained from working with racing aircraft. The services soon were purchasing PW-8–derived versions: The Navy and Marines began buying the Curtiss F6C Hawk fighter in 1925, and the Army purchased the P-1 Hawk version.

Most variants used an in-line water-cooled Curtiss engine. Later versions of the Navy F6C were re-engined with the Pratt & Whitney Wasp radial engine. The Army P-6 variant had an improved engine, the Curtiss V-1570 Conqueror. In the early 1930s, a modified version of the Army P-6 fitted with a radial engine became the Navy F11C Goshawk fighter.   The Curtiss P-1/P-6 series thus became the premier U.S. Army Air Corps fighter of the mid-1920s.   The related F6C Hawk series was less widely used, but it remained an important Navy and Marine fighter of the 1920s (Green and Swanborough, 1994).

Boeing

As with Curtiss, the Boeing Company got its start with seaplanes when, in 1915, William E. Boeing and Navy Commander Conrad Westervelt of Seattle formed a partnership to develop a new seaplane.   Boeing's first extensive experience with land-based fighters came shortly after World War I, when the Seattle firm won most of the production contract for the Thomas-Morse MB-3A fighter, beating out the much more experienced Thomas-Morse Aircraft Corporation, which had designed the aircraft.   The MB-3A design was itself a derivative of the French SPAD.   Its engine was an "Americanized" French Hispano-Suiza (Bowers, 1989).   Through the production of the MB-3A, Boeing would become the other dominant fighter developer and producer in the 1920s.   Boeing had neither developed the fighter nor did it possess the engineering capability to do so.   Thomas-Morse, which had engineered the technology development and innovations that led to this reasonably successful fighter, was ruined financially by the government's selection of Boeing for the production contract.

The experience gained from the manufacture of the MB-3A led Boeing to develop its own fighter design-engineering capabilities. Using its own company funds, Boeing began developing its own fighter designs.[8] The resulting Boeing Model 15 proved successful. It was procured in small though significant numbers throughout the mid-1920s by the Army, as the PW-9 series, and by the Navy, as the FB-1 series.

---

[8]According to Vander Meulen (1991), Boeing was quite an exception in this respect. Vander Meulen claims that, for the most part, producing aircraft designed by other firms did little to promote the development of design expertise within the production firms. At the same time, he claims that such practices led to poorly manufactured aircraft and reduced incentives among contractors to invest in R&D and maintain design-engineering staffs.

Now established as a recognized fighter developer, Boeing took on as its next effort the F2B fighter for the Navy. Developed in 1926, the F2B airframe was a close derivative of the FB-1 series, re-engined with a Pratt & Whitney Wasp power plant.

The most successful fighter of the 1920s and early 1930s started as a Boeing Company venture called the Model 83 and Model 89. Tested by service pilots in 1928, this fighter was purchased by the Army as the P-12 series and the Navy as the F4B series, becoming their respective standard fighters in the early 1930s. Variants of this same basic design were procured in large numbers (by U.S. inter-war standards). Boeing manufactured nearly 600 aircraft of this same design group, making the P-12/F4B series the most heavily procured U.S. fighter between 1918 and the onset of massive U.S. rearmament in 1940.

Yet the highly successful P-12/F4B design series was extremely conservative and used the same Pratt & Whitney Wasp engine as both its Boeing and Curtiss predecessors. Bowers' comprehensive history of Boeing aircraft describes the P-12/F4B series as follows (1989, p. 162):

> There was nothing really new about the new design, except the model number. . . . [It] used only conservative and thoroughly-tested features.

The design philosophy behind the P-12/F4B series was similar to that behind Boeing's major contender for the Postal Service airmail market, the Model 40, designed a few years earlier. According to Heppenheimer's authoritative history of commercial aviation industry (1995, p. 15),

> [I]n their technical design, airplanes in the 1920s were generally failing to advance . . . One could see this in the Boeing 40 of 1927, built a decade after the war. It had its air-cooled engine, but in other respects its layout remained thoroughly conventional. It showed a fuselage framework built of welded steel tubes, a construction technique that dated to 1916. Other features included the usual: open cockpit, biplane wings with ribs of spruce, fabric covering . . . . This stodginess in design contrasted sharply with the great freedom available to designers.

U.S. BOMBER DEVELOPMENT DURING THE BIPLANE ERA

Because of the very small government demand and limited opportunities on the export market, the number of U.S. firms focusing on the bomber market in the 1920s and early 1930s was even more restricted than in the fighter/pursuit aircraft arena. Essentially two companies dominated the design of heavy bombers during this period: Martin and Keystone.

Glenn L. Martin dominated the first generation of heavy bomber designs. However, because the government split production from design by competitively sourcing the production contracts, Martin lost significant amounts of money on its most successful design. As a result, Martin effectively withdrew from the bomber market throughout the remainder of the 1920s (Vander Meulen, 1991). In the late 1920s and early 1930s, Keystone dominated bomber design. Martin and Keystone produced designs that were robust but conservative, even pedestrian. They were not high-risk innovators.

The low demand after the war was exacerbated by the large number of excess existing bombers on the market. After entering the war, the U.S. government developed plans to license-produce over 12,000 British-developed De Havilland DH-4 observation planes/bombers, with Boeing as the prime contractor. Although these plans were slashed after the Armistice, nearly 5,000 such bombers were produced by 1919. Thus, large numbers of foreign-designed bombers remained in the U.S. Army inventory throughout most of the 1920s, further suppressing the U.S. market for new bombers.[9] Furthermore, the DH-4 was obsolete even at the time it went into production in the United States. Therefore, it was fairly easy for U.S. contractors to develop an indigenous design that surpassed the DH-4's capabilities without taking great risks with new technologies or innovations.

The first successful heavy two-engine bomber of any type designed and built in the United States (Taylor, 1995), the MB-1, was developed by the Glenn L. Martin Company during the last days of the

---

[9]Up to ten contractors and Army Air Corps depots were kept busy during the early and mid-1920s, upgrading and remanufacturing the obsolete DH-4s. The most significant upgrade program involved the DH-4M variant manufactured by Boeing and Atlantic (Fokker) in 1923 and 1924. See Swanborough (1963).

war.[10] Glenn Martin established the company in Cleveland in 1917. Later specializing in large seaplanes, Martin's first major contract came from the U.S. Army for the development of a U.S. heavy bomber, which exceeded the capabilities of the British Handley Page 0/400, then in production under license in the United States. The Martin MB-1 began development in early 1918 and first flew during the summer.

The Army bought small numbers of MB-1 variants for the bomber and reconnaissance roles. The Navy also procured the TM-1 version for the torpedo/bomber mission. Another variant entered the Postal Service inventory as an airmail carrier.

In 1920, the Army began procuring a total of about 125 examples of different variants of the improved Martin MB-2/NBS-1 versions. In typical fashion, the Army competitively outsourced production. Curtiss, not Martin, built the bulk (50) of the procured MB-2/NBS-1 variants. In addition, both Aeromarine and LWF built more of these bombers than did Martin. Along with the remaining DH-4 bombers license-produced by Boeing, the Martin MB-2/NBS-1 was a key component of the U.S. Army heavy bomber force throughout most of the 1920s. The MB-2/NBS-1 remained the dominant Army Air Corps bomber from 1921 through 1927 (Munson, 1970b; Swanborough, 1963, and Donald, 1999).

The most important indigenous U.S. Army Air Corps (USAAC)[11] bomber in the 1920s was originally developed by the Huff-Daland Company, which later became the Keystone Aircraft Corporation. The Keystone bombers were intended initially to replace the Martin MB-2/NBS-1 bombers. The Army procured significant quantities of at least nine major twin-engine models of the Keystone LB (B-3A through B-6) bomber series, beginning with the LB-1 in 1927. Production of this reasonably capable but utterly conventional bomber, sporting a World War I standard configuration, continued well into 1932. Indeed, during 1931 and 1932 alone, the USAAC accepted more than 100 of these bombers, for a total procurement of

---

[10]Years later, Martin was incorporated into Martin-Marietta and finally Lockheed-Martin, although it ceased aircraft development activities in 1960.

[11]The Air Corps Act of July 1926 changed the name of the U.S. Army Air Service to the U.S. Army Air Corps (USAAC).

more than 230. Facing little competition from Martin designs or any others, Keystone bombers became the backbone of the USAAC heavy bombardment units by the late 1920s and early 1930s (Taylor, 1995).

SUMMARY: AN ERA OF CONSERVATIVE DESIGNS AND LITTLE INNOVATION

We have seen that both the U.S. fighter and bomber markets in the 1920s and early 1930s could be characterized as having low demand and small procurement numbers, little design competition, few firms seriously competing for military contracts, extremely conservative designs, and very little significant innovation. The most numerous and most recently procured fighters and bombers in the Army Air Corps and Navy inventories in the early 1930s differed little in basic design configuration, construction, and materials from the standards that were well established by 1916. The combat aircraft developed by U.S. industry and procured by the Army Air Corps and Navy for nearly a decade and a half after the end of World War I demonstrated only modest improvements in basic performance relative to the best fighters developed by the Europeans in the late stages of the war, as Table 2.1 demonstrates.

The table compares basic data on the Boeing P-12E, the most modern important fighter coming into the USAAC inventory in 1932, with data on the SPAD S.XIII, the French fighter flown by Capt. Eddie Rickenbacker in 1918 and that equipped the 94th Aero Pursuit Squadron on the Western Front. The Boeing fighter shows important performance improvements over the SPAD—a 35-percent improvement in top speed, a 20-percent reduction in climb time to 5,000 ft, and around a 23-percent improvement in both service ceiling and useful payload. It is clearly superior.

However, these gains in performance are not *revolutionary*, given the nearly decade and a half that separates the development of the two aircraft. Recall how numerous were the incrementally improved designs, models, and variants that preceded the Boeing P-12E. On average, the numbers in Table 2.1 show an annual compounded performance improvement of from approximately 1.7 percent to 2.5

Table 2.1

Incremental Improvement: SPAD S.XIII Versus Boeing P-12E

Aircraft Characteristic	SPAD S.XIII	Boeing P-12E
First flight	4 April 1917	15 October 1931
Configuration	Single seat, open cockpit, fixed landing gear, biplane	Single seat, open cockpit, fixed landing gear, biplane
Structure, materials	Wood structure, fabric skin	Bolted/welded metal tubes and wood structure, fabric with some metal skins
Maximum speed	139 mph @ 6,560 ft	189 mph @ 7,000 ft
Climb time to 5,000 ft	200 sec (approx.)	162 sec (F4B-4)
Service ceiling	21,815 ft	26,900 ft
Empty weight	1,326 lb	1,999 lb
Loaded weight	1,888 lb	2,690 lb
Armament	2 forward-firing 7.7mm machine guns	2 forward-firing 7.62mm machine guns

percent. Compared with the performance improvements witnessed during the initial decade of aircraft development and the first period of revolutionary combat-aircraft development (1909–1916), as well as the later monoplane revolution (1931–1940) and other later eras of rapid technological innovation, this improvement is modest indeed.

What explains this lack of innovation and design conservatism from the late teens to the early 1930s? We believe that, at least in part, it was likely caused by the relative lack of competition in military air-craft development, owing to the very small number of experienced, financially viable, and technologically credible firms competing for bomber and fighter contracts. This small number was, in turn, caused primarily by the low demand from and the small size of the domestic market. It is difficult to decisively prove this correlation with the available evidence, however.

To further shed light on the question of innovation during this period, we turn in the next chapter to an examination of what elements seemed to cause this situation to change dramatically, leading to the period of very high innovation in both bombers and fighters that began early in the 1930s.

Chapter Three

THE MONOPLANE REVOLUTION

After years of technology and design stagnation characterized by persistent retention of the basic airframe/engine configuration already well established by 1916, combat aircraft entered a period of revolutionary advancement in technology and design configuration at the beginning of the 1930s. What changes in the demand and the supply side of the military aircraft market, and in the structure of the aircraft industry, are correlated with the emergence of this technology revolution after so many years of stagnation? This chapter identifies those changes.

NEW MARKETS AND GREATER COMPETITION PAVE THE WAY FOR INNOVATION

The monoplane revolution, which began in earnest in the early 1930s, was driven by a change in attitude and approach by contractors responding to new market conditions. The most important cause of this change was a transformation in perception: of the potential future sales opportunities offered, first by the commercial market and later, and more important (from our perspective), by the anticipated growth of the global military market. The first major breakthroughs came in the commercial market. Responding to the birth of a viable commercial airline industry, demand emerged for a new generation of high-performance passenger transport aircraft. The new demand stimulated new entrants into the industry to meet those requirements, and stimulated marked new competition and innovation.

The new technologies and designs pioneered in response to the emergence of the new commercial market were soon applied to military combat aircraft. The first dual-use area for commercial applications was in bomber aircraft. Again, newcomers entered the military market in response to a perception of increased market opportunities, which, in turn, led to greater competition for military contracts and stimulated much greater innovation in military aircraft.

The military application and further development of revolutionary technologies and new design concepts first developed for the commercial market accelerated dramatically in the early 1930s in response to another perception: Market opportunities were increasing with the outbreak of warfare in the Far East and the destabilization of Europe with the rise of Fascism and National Socialism.

The most innovative firms in the military market (as well as in the commercial market) tended to be new entrants or established aviation firms entering new market sectors. U.S. government demand for military combat remained uncertain and relatively low until the massive rearmament program of 1940–1941, as shown in Figures 3.1 and 3.2. The new, highly innovative companies tended to look toward exports and the global market to shore up uncertain U.S. government demand for military aircraft. This focus required them to compete with long-established, technologically advanced foreign firms. To gain a competitive edge vis-à-vis the established competitors, they were even more inclined to incorporate advanced technologies and novel approaches in their designs.[1]

The crucial motivating factor in the commercial market was the reduction in government subsidies for airmail, especially after the congressional Waters Act of 1930.[2] This policy change had major implications for the fledgling U.S. commercial airline industry, which up until this time depended primarily on the heavily government-subsidized airmail market to provide its main source of profits. The established airlines recognized that they needed to focus more on

---

[1]The European Airbus consortium in the 1980s adopted this same strategy to help break the stranglehold that Boeing had on the commercial wide-body-jet transport market.

[2]Formally the McNary-Waters Act of 1930, this act cut the airmail rates in half and gave the Postmaster General total control over airmail routes.

passenger service to remain economically viable. To compete with railroads and other modes of transportation for both the now-more-deregulated mail market *and* the passenger market, the airlines realized that they needed to acquire higher-speed, larger, more-comfortable, and more-cost-effective civil passenger transport aircraft.

Equipping civil transports with such capabilities required contractors to integrate new and untested technologies into radically different kinds of high-risk aircraft designs. Contractors were willing to do so now because a new commercial airliner market that had not existed in the 1920s was emerging and because a new global military-aircraft market began to appear that could benefit enormously from dual-use commercial technologies. Although important new technologies and design concepts had been developed independently during the 1920s, most aircraft firms were unwilling to take the financial risks of applying the new technologies and designs and integrating them into new aircraft before the Waters Act deregulated airmail and provided greater economic incentives for the airlines and their aircraft suppliers to take greater risks. The emergence of the new market demand brought in many new contractors, greatly intensifying the competition and placing a much greater premium on technological innovation for winning market share, in both new markets, commercial and military.

Continuing from where Figure 2.2 leaves off, with a commercial market just emerging from being totally overshadowed by the military market, in the late 1920s, Figure 3.1 shows the new importance of the commercial market for aircraft manufacturers. Commercial-aircraft production significantly surpassed military aircraft production throughout the 1930s, but particularly at the beginning of the decade, when it was crucial for stimulating the takeoff of the monoplane revolution, and then again at the end of the decade, before massive U.S. rearmament was launched in 1940. During the leanest Depression years, 1932 through 1935, commercial aircraft sales, although much reduced from those of the preceding four years, remained valued at more than military aircraft sales, and thus helped the aircraft industry weather the severe economic downturn.

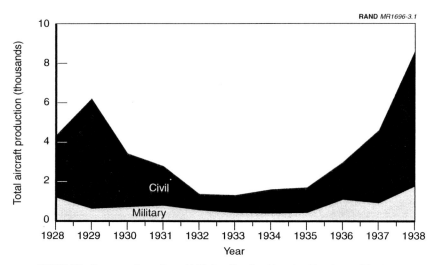

SOURCE: Data are from Donald M. Pattillo, *Pushing the Envelope: The American Aircraft Industry*, Ann Arbor, Michigan: The University of Michigan Press, 2000, Table 9.

Figure 3.1—U.S. Military and Commercial Aircraft Production, 1928–1938

Figure 3.2 shows how overall Army and Navy air appropriations declined in the mid-1930s, remaining at a low level until at least 1935. After 1935, air appropriations began rising steadily, thus further stimulating the military aircraft market. Nonetheless, they remained at relatively modest levels, forcing military aircraft contractors to depend heavily on foreign sales, as discussed in the section "Markets, Competition, and Innovation During the Monoplane Revolution" later in this chapter.

Given these demand trends, it is not surprising that technological entrepreneurs and venture capitalists outside of the established military aircraft industry were the first to launch the new era of high innovation for aircraft in the 1920s that led to the monoplane revolution. Such entrepreneurs included Jack Northrop, Allan Loughead, and Donald Douglas. These men saw the new potential commercial value of developing faster, more-efficient airliners.

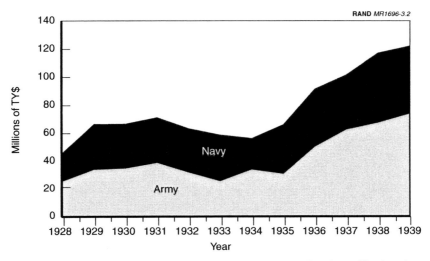

SOURCE: Data are from Donald M. Pattillo, *Pushing the Envelope: The American Aircraft Industry*, Ann Arbor, Michigan: The University of Michigan Press, 2000, Table 8.

NOTE: *Air appropriations* include other procurement and other expenditures in addition to the procurement of aircraft.

Figure 3.2—U.S. Army and Navy Air Appropriations, 1928–1939

Supported by venture capitalists, Loughead established the Lockheed Aircraft Corporation in 1926 in Los Angeles.[3] He employed Jack Northrop to develop a radical new airliner design, the Lockheed Vega. The Vega was a highly streamlined high-speed design with a single, unbraced wing at the bottom of the fuselage—a design that departed drastically from existing conventional high-wing designs, such as the lumbering Ford and Fokker trimotor civil transports then dominating civil air travel. The Vega, which first flew in 1927, proved to be reasonably successful commercially by the standards of the time (Heppenheimer, 1995; Anderson, 1976; and Yenne, 1980).

It took the emergence of potentially new and lucrative markets to spur innovators to take the financial and technological risks of

---

[3]Annoyed with the mispronunciation and misspelling of his name, Loughead changed his name to Lockheed.

integrating the component technologies that had been around for some time into new aircraft designs. Such technologies included the long-known concept of "stressed skin" construction for lighter wings; the development of much more powerful and lighter air-cooled radial engines;[4] the invention of the "NACA cowl,"[5] which led to the streamlining of engines; the development of a new and better type of aluminum; retractable landing gear; and enclosed cockpits. Lockheed's Jack Northrop integrated most of these elements into another new commercial design called the Alpha, which first flew in March 1930. At about the same time, Boeing began developing a new high-speed airmail and transport plane called the Monomail, using the same radical design approach and technologies (Heppenheimer, 1995).

In 1930, Boeing was the most successful fighter developer and manufacturer in the United States. Its new interest in a cutting-edge all-metal monoplane was of great importance to the military. While less-radical commercial high-wing, all-metal monoplanes such as the Ford and Fokker trimotors had become commonplace in the airliner and airmail markets, monoplanes of any type were nonexistent in the U.S. combat aircraft market. In 1928, Boeing began development, with company funds, of an all-metal monoplane fighter prototype called the XP-9. However, this aircraft remained technologically behind the leading commercial designs such as the Lockheed Vega and Alpha. The XP-9, which did not fly until 1930, exhibited disappointing performance and was not procured. But it spurred Boeing's interest in developing the more radical Monomail Model 200/221 for the commercial market. This all-metal single-engine monoplane first flew in May 1930. Highly streamlined and equipped with retractable landing gear, it proved to be a modest commercial success (Bowers, 1989). It would provide the basic learning for the development of a revolutionary bomber design.

---

[4]Such engine development was supported partly by U.S. Navy funding.

[5]The National Advisory Committee for Aeronautics (NACA) was the predecessor of the National Aeronautics and Space Administration (NASA).

THE MONOPLANE BOMBER REVOLUTION

For over a decade following World War I, little fundamental innovation had taken place in the basic performance, configuration, and technology of bombers. Then, in a brief period of two years or so in the early 1930s, streamlined, twin-engine, all-metal, low-wing monoplane bombers with retractable landing gear and enclosed cockpits were flown, tested, and designated for procurement in Germany, Russia, and the United Kingdom, as well as in the United States. Indeed, U.S. industry clearly led the way in the monoplane bomber revolution.

Ironically, the Army Air Corps procurement establishment during this period has been accused of extreme technological conservatism. Yet, by the late 1920s, the Air Corps, aware of the new developments in the commercial transport market, was already gaining interest in investigating more-advanced monoplane designs for bombers. In 1930, the Army Air Corps test-flew numerous examples of the Y1B-7 bomber. A fairly conservatively designed all-metal, high-wing monoplane bomber developed by Douglas Aircraft, the Y1B-7 was not technologically radically different from the existing high-wing passenger airliners of the period. The USAAC also evaluated the General Aviation (Fokker) XB-8 monoplane bomber prototype (Taylor, 1995; Bowers, 1989).

These actions encouraged Boeing to believe that the USAAC might be receptive to the application of truly revolutionary designs and technologies derived from its Monomail design and other cutting-edge commercial transports to a new Army bomber. As a result, in 1930 Boeing invested its own money in the development of a new bomber prototype, the Y1B-9, which drew heavily on the new technologies and design lessons learned from the XP-9 and the Monomail Model 200.

The Y1B-9 is widely considered to have revolutionized bomber design in the United States, if not the world. It was an all-metal, two-engine, semi-monocoque, cantilever low-wing monoplane with retractable landing gear. The first prototype, which flew in April 1931, far outperformed existing biplane bombers. Even more impressive, it flew 5 mph faster than the quickest fighter (pursuit aircraft) in the Army Air Corps inventory. The USAAC began service-testing of the

Y1B-9 in July 1932. Although the senior service leadership was ex- tremely impressed with the Boeing aircraft, a slightly newer and even more capable bomber prototype soon caught their attention (Taylor, 1982; Bowers, 1989; Heppenheimer, 1995).

As noted in Chapter Two, Martin's MB-2/NBS-1 bomber was the first successful U.S. indigenous bomber design, forming the backbone of the Army Air Corps bomber force from 1921 through 1927. However, in the late 1920s and early 1930s, Martin had remained out of the bomber market, which was dominated by the Keystone LB bomber series, the replacement for the MB-2/NBS-1. With the emergence of new potential market opportunities, Martin decided to risk re- entering the bomber market, despite its unhappy experience with the outsourcing of production of the MB-2/NBS-1 bomber to other con- tractors. Martin spent corporate money to develop its own highly advanced bomber prototype, the Martin Model 123 (XB-907), aimed at providing a replacement for the Keystone LB bombers.

The Air Corps began proof-testing the XB-907 in mid-1932. As with the Boeing Y1B-9, the XB-907 integrated many of the new technolog- ical and design innovations that were beginning to be applied to ad- vanced commercial transport aircraft. Later designated the XB-10, the Martin prototype was an all-metal, cantilever mid-wing mono- plane with retracting landing gear. However, it boasted two signifi- cant improvements over the Boeing Y1B-9: internal bomb carriage and the first enclosed gun turret ever mounted on a U.S. bomber. Perhaps most important, it was more than 10 mph faster than the fastest test version of the Boeing bomber. To Boeing's bitter disap- pointment, the Army ordered the Martin B-10 into production in January 1933, ultimately procuring nearly 160 of the aircraft (Swanborough, 1963; Donald, 1999). The B-10's dramatic improve- ment over the existing generation of bombers is shown in Table 3.1.

First appearing in the United States, the bomber monoplane revolu- tion quickly spread to several other countries that were experiencing similar expansions in commercial market demand, along with much stronger growth than the United States in the domestic military market. Most of the initial foreign designs originally were aimed

Table 3.1

Biplane Versus Monoplane Bomber Performance

Performance Measure	Keystone B-6A	Boeing Y1B-9	Martin Model 166 (B-10)
First flight	28 April 1931[a]	13 April 1931	20 April 1932[b]
Maximum speed (mph)	121	174	207
Range (mi)	825	1,250	2,080

SOURCE: Data are from Peter M. Bowers, *Boeing Aircraft Since 1916*, Annapolis, Md.: Naval Institute Press, 1989; Michael J. H. Taylor, ed., *Jane's Encyclopedia of Aviation*, New York: Crescent Books, 1995; Glenn L. Martin Aviation Museum, *Martin Aircraft Specifications*, Middle River, Md., 1998.

[a]Award of USAAC production contract.

[b]Martin XB-907.

at either the commercial airmail or passenger markets. Although the foreign designs first flew slightly later than the initial U.S. designs, the European bombers were often more advanced in several respects, partly in response to the more robust domestic military demand for combat aircraft emerging in foreign countries.[6]

The competition between the Boeing B-9 and Martin B-10 is important in the U.S. context for several reasons:

• It demonstrates that failure to buy advanced-technology combat aircraft was not caused primarily by hidebound conservatism in the Army Air Corps leadership, as is often alleged.

• To the contrary, procurement of the B-10 represented the first large-scale sale and production of the radical new cantilever low-wing, all-metal monoplane aircraft design for any type of customer in the United States, including commercial customers.

---

[6]The Heinkel He 70 (first flight, December 1932) and the Dornier Do 17 (first flight, fall 1934) were originally conceived as civil transports, as was the Bristol 135, predecessor of the Blenheim bomber (first flight, April 1935). From its inception, the Russian Tupolev SB-2 (first flight, October 1934) was designed as a bomber.

- As noted in Chapter Two, the USAAC actually led the entire world by supporting development and procurement of the first bombers of this type.

The key to the monoplane revolution in the United States, as well as in the United Kingdom and pre-Nazi Germany, was the perception that there was a large enough dual-use market to justify the risks involved in integrating the new technologies, almost all of which were already known and had been tested separately. The U.S. Army Air Corps alone did not represent a large enough or reliable enough market to justify the development risk by contractors, particularly since the USAAC was not inclined to pay fully for the R&D costs of developing a prototype, and could still outsource production to other contractors. It is crucial to remember that both the Boeing B-9 and the Martin B-10 were developed with company venture capital. To justify such expenditure and risk, multiple markets had to be identified.

As noted earlier in this chapter, two new markets in addition to the Army Air Corps bomber market were crucial to spurring the new spate of innovation: the commercial air transport market and the military export market.

As Heppenheimer (1995) emphasizes, the congressional Waters Act of 1930 greatly reduced the government subsidy to commercial carriers for airmail, thus forcing the airlines to focus more on passengers and on more-efficient delivery of the mail. This new focus resulted in an increased demand for much faster, more cost-effective transport aircraft, encouraging Jack Northrop at Lockheed to improve his Lockheed Vega design and come out with the new Alpha in 1930. It also spurred Boeing to develop its Monomail Model 200. Fortuitously, the same size aircraft, the same desired performance parameters, and the same technologies were equally applicable to the commercial passenger and mail-delivery markets as to the USAAC bomber market—and were enormously important to spurring the monoplane revolution in bombers.

Thus, it is no accident that the monoplane revolution took place first with bombers rather than fighters. Bomber technology in this era was clearly dual-use. Technology developed for bombers was directly applicable to commercial passenger and cargo transports, and vice versa. Indeed, after losing the bomber contract to the Martin XB-10, Boeing went ahead and directly applied the technical experience gained on the Monomail and Y1B-9 programs to developing the Model 247. The Model 247 evolved into the world's first truly successful modern passenger transport. United Airlines' purchase of the Model 247 made it the leading U.S. passenger airline.

The two-way dual-use flow of technology and design expertise is clearly demonstrated by Douglas. Douglas had long experience in developing Navy bombers and other large military aircraft. In response to United Airlines' great success with the acquisition of Boeing's Model 247, TWA sent a letter to other aircraft manufacturers proposing the development of a competitive airliner. The dominant airliner manufacturer of the time, General Aviation (which built technologically conservative Dutch Fokker high-wing trimotors in the United States), was unable to come up with a suitable advanced design. Douglas Aircraft, principally a builder of large conventional Navy torpedo bombers and Army utility aircraft, responded with its radical DC-1 design, which incorporated many of the revolutionary new design and technology features developed for the Vega, Alpha, Monomail, B-9, Model 247, and B-10. Indeed, one of its principal designers was Jack Northrop, who had left Lockheed. Donald Douglas himself had much bomber experience, having formerly been the chief engineer in charge of the Martin MB-2/NBS-1 bomber program. The DC-1 evolved quickly into the DC-3, the most successful and most famous commercial transport of the prop era.[7]

In spite of the dual-use nature of bomber technology and designs, the development of high-risk innovative new-technology bombers in the United States would probably not have taken place without the perception of a new and growing foreign global market in high-performance bombers. Significantly, the gathering war clouds overseas implied a newly invigorated foreign market for combat aircraft to supplement uncertain and relatively low U.S. government demand for bombers. The Japanese Army coup in Manchuria took place in 1931, which led to the Sino-Japanese War. Mussolini was clearly pushing Italy into an expansionist posture by the early 1930s, and the Weimar Republic was staggering under a Nazi and

---

[7]Later, as the C-47, it became the most famous military transport of the era.

Communist political onslaught. Hitler was finally appointed Chancellor in January 1933, followed shortly thereafter by the beginnings of massive German rearmament and a new armaments race in Europe. Many military planners, as well as the popular press of the time, viewed a new generation of high-performance bombers as the pivotal weapon of the next war.

With the prospects for war in both Europe and Asia clearly growing, while isolationism remained dominant on the U.S. political scene, it is not surprising that Martin ended up selling more B-10s on the global market than it sold to the U.S. government. Indeed, the Netherlands alone purchased 120 B-10s, most for use in the Dutch Pacific possessions to counter the Japanese. The Dutch procurement of B-10s alone nearly equaled that of the USAAC.

Thus, radical new bomber innovation preceded fighter innovation in the United States as well as in foreign countries, in large part because the dual-use nature of bomber designs reduced the economic risk for contractors. But the military market for both bombers and fighters still remained small and uncertain in the United States until 1940. Only when the overseas military market appeared sufficiently lucrative, and only after the basic technologies had been tested first on commercial transport and then on bomber designs, did the monoplane revolution overtake the fighter market.

THE MONOPLANE FIGHTER REVOLUTION

The first operational single-seat, cantilever low-wing, monocoque fighter with retractable landing gear did not fly until December 1933, three and a half years after the Boeing Monomail Model 200 and more than six years after the first flight of the Lockheed Vega. Moreover, unlike advanced bombers of the era, this fighter, the stubby I-16, was not the result of private enterprise but was developed by the Russian Polikarpov design house and funded by the Soviet state (Green and Swanborough, 1994).

Fighter design and technology did not have the same commercial applications as bomber technology; therefore, U.S. firms were slower to focus on the fighter segment. U.S. companies may have led the world during at least the initial phases of the monoplane bomber revolution, because the United States had one of the most aggressive, market-oriented commercial airline markets in the world, especially compared with the heavily regulated and subsidized European airlines. Thus, U.S. contractors had strong market incentives to develop both new-technology civil transports and bombers.

On the other hand, militaristic European governments, such as the Hitler and Stalin regimes, appear to have been more willing and able than the U.S. government to subsidize the development of advanced monoplane fighters (whose designs and performance had far less dual-use application to the commercial transport market). Thus, although U.S. industry pioneered the monoplane revolution in bombers, it lagged behind the Germans, Soviets, British, and, later, the Japanese in the initial development and refinement of the monoplane fighter. Without a U.S. domestic dual-use commercial market for fighter monoplane technology, U.S. contractors had to depend entirely on sales to foreign governments to supplement the low and uncertain U.S. government demand for fighters. Without the demand and competition provided by the international fighter market, there is little doubt that U.S. fighter designs and technology would have been even further behind foreign developments at the time of Pearl Harbor than they in fact were.

By 1931, both the U.S. Army Air Corps and the Navy had become seriously interested in developing a modern monoplane fighter; however, they did not heavily subsidize its development. Late in the year, Boeing won a partial USAAC contract to complete development of a company-funded monoplane fighter design. Reflecting its desire to reduce technological risk in this more uncertain market, Boeing produced a fighter design that was far more conservative than the Monomail of 1930 or the Y1B-9 bomber prototype. While drawing heavily on the earlier transport and bomber designs, the resulting P-26A sported old-fashioned fixed landing gear and only partial cantilever wire-braced wings.

Nonetheless, the Army selected the P-26A at the end of 1933, ordering 111 aircraft—the largest single fighter contract since 1921. Already surpassed by existing bomber and transport technology before it even flew, the P-26A Peashooter remained the USAAC frontline fighter until it began its phase-out in the 1938–1940 period. Boeing also developed the more-advanced YP-29 fighter technology demonstrators and a Navy cousin, the XF7B-1, but neither was procured because of disappointing performance (Bowers, 1989).

It took an enterprising Russian émigré designer and his fledgling company to take the design and technology risks to offer the Army Air Corps its first truly modern cantilever low-wing fighter with retractable landing gear. The Navy acquired its equivalent fighter from a long-established company that had only recently entered the aircraft market because of the perceived new global-market opportunities.

In May 1935, the USAAC Material Division issued a requirement for an advanced monoplane fighter. In 1931, Soviet émigré Alexander P. Seversky and his chief designer Alexander Kartveli had established the Seversky Aircraft Corporation, which later became Republic Aircraft. The company funded two advanced prototype fighters for the Air Corps: the SEV-1XP and 2XP (Stoff, 1990). Submitted to the Army for trials, the 1XP competed fiercely against the Curtiss Model 75, another company-funded test vehicle developed by one of the old leaders in fighter development. The upstart Seversky aircraft won in April 1936, but the Army required changes to the design before awarding the production contract. Redesigned by Kartveli, the 1XP became the AP-1, resulting in the first USAAC all-metal, cantilever low-wing fighter with retractable landing gear. It was also the first with an enclosed cockpit and variable propeller. While only a relatively mediocre performer, the P-35 (production version of AP-1) later evolved into the dramatically improved P-47 Thunderbolt, the most-produced American fighter of World War II (Jones, 1975).[8]

The Navy issued its specification for a modern monoplane fighter in 1936. With its XFN-1 design, Seversky competed against the relatively new Grumman company and its XF4F-1 biplane design. Meanwhile, Brewster Aeronautical Corporation submitted its XF2A-1 proposal. The Brewster Company was founded in 1810 to manufacture carriages, and entered the aircraft business as a prime con-

---

[8]First flown in May 1935, the German Messerschmitt Bf-109B was the first truly modern all-metal, stressed-skin, monocoque, single-seat fighter to enter active operational service. The first production-standard Bf-109B was completed in early 1937, months before the award of the first P-35 production contract. See Green and Swanborough (1994).

tractor only in 1935. No successful proposals were received from the former industry leaders, Boeing and Curtiss. Instead, the upstart Brewster F2A Buffalo won the competition in June 1936, becoming the Navy's first modern monoplane shipborne fighter. As a backup in case the high-risk monoplane technology failed, the Navy also approved further development of the Grumman XF4F-1 biplane design, which later evolved into the Grumman XF4F-2 monoplane proposal, eventually becoming one of the most famous Navy fighters of World War II: the F4F Wildcat.

Table 3.2 shows some of the performance improvements in fighters achieved by the monoplane technology revolution.

Table 3.2

Advanced Biplane Versus Early Land- and Sea-Based Monoplane Fighter Performance

Performance Measure	Boeing P-12E	Seversky SEV-1XP (P-35)	Brewster B-239 (F2A-1)
First flight	15 October 1931	June 1933[a]	December 1937
Maximum speed (mph)	189	289	301
Rate of climb (ft/min)	1,852 (F4B-4)	2,440[b]	3,060
Service ceiling (ft)	26,900	31,400[b]	33,200[c]

[a]SEV-3.

[b]P-35.

[c]F2A-3.

MARKETS, COMPETITION, AND INNOVATION DURING THE MONOPLANE REVOLUTION

Almost all the winning designs, as well as losing designs and prototypes, in both the Army and Navy competitions for the new-technology monoplane fighters were partially or fully company-financed. Companies were willing to take major risks in the 1930s that they avoided in the 1920s, because the export market was projected to become more robust and because most of the basic technologies had been tested out because of dual-use applications to commercial transports and bombers.

In the United States, the existence of a growing foreign market was absolutely crucial for contractor development of advanced-technology fighters.[9] For example, while the Army Air Corps procured a mere 77 Seversky P-35As, the Swedish government bought 120 improved export versions called the EP-106/J9. The U.S. Navy bought a total of 205 Brewster Buffaloes, 44 of which were diverted to the Finnish government. Yet Brewster received orders for more than 300 Buffaloes from the United Kingdom, the Netherlands, and Belgium. The company-funded Curtiss Hawk 75, which lost the USAAC competition to the Seversky P-35, continued to be tested by the Army, and was ordered into production in 1937 as the P-36A. Slightly more than 200 were ordered, at the time the largest single fighter contract since World War I. However, a grand total of roughly 1,300 of this fighter aircraft and its variants were eventually manufactured, the vast majority exported to France, the UK, and other overseas customers. Indeed, the Curtiss P-36 Hawk was the second-most-numerous combat aircraft in the French inventory at the time of the German invasion in 1940 (Gunston, 1978a; Swanborough, 1963; Donald, 1999).

Economic data support this anecdotal information. As shown in Figure 3.3, U.S. industry foreign sales began increasing as early as 1932. U.S. Army and Navy aviation procurement did not stop declining and begin increasing until 1935. Even more telling, total U.S. aviation industry exports significantly exceeded total U.S. Army and Navy aviation procurement for the years 1939 through 1941, and almost certainly also for 1938.[10]

The crucial role played by the export market, particularly for military combat aircraft, enhanced competition and promoted greater innovation among U.S. contractors. To succeed in the global market, U.S.

---

[9]According to Vander Meulen (1991, p. 188), "Exports during the 1930s provided solid profits that allowed the industry at least marginal viability under Congress's regulatory framework." According to estimates quoted in Vander Meulen, 80 percent of industry profits and two-thirds of development costs came from export sales.

[10]According to Vander Meulen (1991), the data for 1938 are not available.

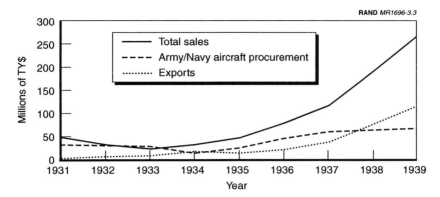

SOURCE: Data are from Jacob A. Vander Meulen, *The Politics of Aircraft: Building an American Military Industry*, Lawrence, Kansas: University Press of Kansas, 1991.

NOTE: *Total sales* and *exports* include all finished military and commercial aircraft, engines, parts, and other aircraft-related articles. Army/Navy aircraft procurement numbers are inflated because items other than aircraft-industry products are included. Data for 1938 are unavailable. Data points shown for 1938 are an average of 1937 and 1939.

Figure 3.3—Total U.S. Aircraft Industry Sales Compared with Exports and Army/Navy Aircraft Procurement, 1931–1939

firms had to compete with more-experienced and often technologically more advanced foreign firms. Therefore, the only way to succeed was to adopt a strategy of technological innovation and technology leapfrogging.

INDUSTRY STRUCTURE DURING THE MONOPLANE REVOLUTION

In short, a key factor bringing about the change from the technologically stagnant 1920s to the revolutionary innovation of the 1930s was the perception of a dramatic increase in market potential resulting from three factors: the emergence of a potentially robust foreign market, the stirrings of a much more viable civil aircraft market in the United States, and the high technological overlap between commercial transports and combat aircraft, especially bombers. This market expansion drew many new entrants into the combat aircraft market, resulting in intense competition, a competition that appears to have spurred even greater innovation. Many of the basic technological innovations were known in the 1920s, but it took an enlargement of the potential market for companies to accept the risks of integrating them into new designs with their own money. Once the market potential became widely recognized, new entrants joined the fray, intensifying the competition.

The financial data of aircraft manufacturers confirm the existence of a much more competitive aircraft industry structure in the 1930s than in the 1920s. As the data in Figures 2.3 and 2.4 and the ensuing discussion indicate, only two firms—Boeing and Curtiss—dominated the U.S. fighter market in the 1920s, and two other firms—Martin and Keystone—dominated the bomber market.

The 1938 sales data in Figure 3.4 show three very large prime contractors, four smaller prime contractors, and another five important prime contractors. Virtually all these contractors were serious competitors for all U.S. combat aircraft contracts, both for fighters and for bombers. But these data are somewhat misleading for a variety of reasons. First, the numbers aggregate both commercial and military sales. The premier position of Douglas is in great part due to the huge success of its DC-3 commercial passenger transport. Nonetheless, in 1938 Douglas was an extremely active and competitive developer of military aircraft, the most important of which were the B-18 bomber, which was the standard USAAC bomber, and the TBD Devastator, which was the standard U.S. Navy torpedo bomber and the first monoplane selected for carrier use by the U.S. Navy. In short, Douglas was an important combat aircraft competitor, especially for bombers, but its total sales for military aircraft in 1938 were much lower than shown in Figure 3.4.

The second-largest company—United Aircraft Corporation—was a conglomerate with four major subsidiaries: Chance Vought, Sikorsky, Hamilton-Standard Propeller, and Pratt & Whitney Engines. Among these, only the Vought subsidiary was a prime contractor for military aircraft. During the 1930s, Vought was a relatively less important prime contractor, developing and manufacturing two bomber/observation aircraft for the U.S. Navy (SB2U Vindicator and OS2U Kingfisher). Thus, United's sales of military aircraft in 1938 would also be much lower than shown in Figure 3.4.

Curtiss-Wright was probably still the leading producer of combat fighter aircraft in 1938, but its position as a technology and innovation leader was eroding rapidly. Martin was still a significant provider of bombers, fighters, and other combat aircraft. In the 1930s, the next-largest firm, Consolidated, is best known for developing a modestly successful USAAC fighter and perhaps the most successful Navy flying boat of all time: the PBY Catalina.

All the other firms listed in Figure 3.4, with the exception of Boeing, were aggressive, fairly new entrants to the combat aircraft market. Most of them would vastly increase their military aircraft sales totals

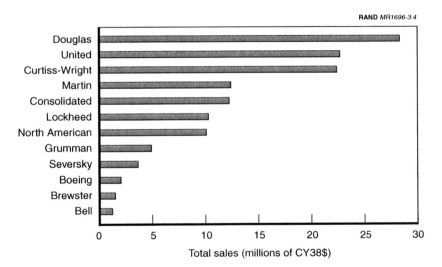

SOURCE: Data are from Jacob A. Vander Meulen, *The Politics of Aircraft: Building an American Military Industry*, Lawrence, Kansas: University Press of Kansas, 1991.

NOTE: The totals for United and Curtiss-Wright are estimates made by Vander Meulen (1991) of total aircraft sales, arrived at by subtracting his estimate of the sales of those companies' large aircraft-engine divisions ($13.3 and $9.7 million, respectively).

Figure 3.4—Total Sales for Top Aircraft Contractors, 1938

over the next several years as large-scale U.S. rearmament began. But the important point here is that, by the mid- to late-1930s, at least 12 credible combat aircraft prime contractors were vigorously competing for both bomber and fighter contracts, whereas only three dominant contractors were competing at any given time in the 1920s.

Perhaps most interesting from our perspective were the eight firms that either were entirely new entrants to the aviation market or had entered into new market sectors in the 1930s, and the roles they played during the period of high innovation during the monoplane technology revolution. Such firms as Lockheed, North American, Seversky, Brewster, Bell, and others, which had never developed a combat aircraft, attempted to break into the new expanding market by resorting to radical and innovative new designs. Table 3.3 summarizes a sample of some of the most notable and innovative U.S. combat aircraft of the monoplane revolution era , indicating whether the firms that developed them were either new entrants or more-experienced companies working outside their area of specialization.

For example, in 1937, Lockheed, which had built its reputation almost entirely on innovative commercial transport aircraft, proposed its first serious military design for a high-altitude interceptor. That design was radical in configuration, armament, and size. It led to the development of the P-38 Lightning, "one of the best known USAAF [U.S. Army Air Force] fighters operational in World War II" (Swanborough, 1963, p. 290).

The North American P-51 Mustang, developed exclusively for the foreign market in 120 days in 1940 by a new company that had never designed a fighter or any other combat aircraft, "became the preeminent long-range escort fighter of World War II and in many respects the greatest all-around combat aircraft" (Taylor, 1995, p. 708). The British originally asked North American to build the Curtiss P-40 under license for the Royal Air Force. The young entrepreneurs at North American countered with an unsolicited proposal to develop their own innovative design, which included an advanced wing design and unique mid-fuselage ventral air intake. The British accepted the offer, changing aviation history.

Table 3.3

New Entrants, Nonspecialists Introduce Key Innovations in the United States, 1930–1940

Aircraft and Innovation	Company and Industry Status[a]
1st Navy fighter with enclosed cockpit, retractable landing gear	**Grumman**
1st monoplane carrier fighter	**Brewster**
1st successful mid-engine fighter	**Bell**
1st USAAC single-seat monoplane fighter with retractable landing gear	**Seversky/Republic**
1st successful twin-engine long-range fighter	*Lockheed*
1st successful twin-engine modern medium bomber	**North American**
1st successful water-cooled in-line engine monoplane fighter	**North American**
1st successful four-engine modern heavy bomber	*Boeing*

[a]**Bold** = New entrant; *italics* = outside area of specialization.

Bell Aircraft, established only in 1935 and trying to break into the market, offered the USAAC and foreign customers several highly unorthodox designs, including the mid-engine P-39. While procured in significant numbers by the USAAC, the P-39 was only a modest success with U.S. forces. However, it became a crucial component of the fighter/attack inventory of the Soviet air force. Nearly 10,000 P-39s were produced, with almost 5,000 going to the Soviet Union.

When North American designed the B-25 Mitchell medium bomber, it was a company with no previous experience in bombers or fighters. This aircraft, which first flew in January 1939, was produced in larger quantities than any other U.S. twin-engine combat aircraft during World War II. According to one observer, it "is often described as the best aircraft in its class in World War II" (Gunston, 1978a).

Boeing, which had dominated the U.S. fighter market from the 1920s through the early 1930s, and which had never sold a bomber to the U.S. government, followed development of its revolutionary but rejected Y1B-9 bomber proposal with an even more radical and innovative bomber design. This aircraft, called the Model 299, was developed at Boeing's own expense in 1935. The prize was an expected large-scale Army Air Corps procurement contract, and possible foreign sales. Boeing took a huge risk by interpreting the Army requirement for a multi-engine aircraft as permitting a four-engine bomber rather than the accepted norm of two engines. The result was a bomber that became possibly one of the most famous combat aircraft of all time: the Boeing B-17 Flying Fortress. Although the company-funded prototype was destroyed during flight-testing by the Army, its performance was so impressive that the Army ordered 13 more test aircraft. Eventually, nearly 13,000 B-17s were built (Bowers, 1989; Swanborough, 1963).

SUMMARY

The U.S. combat aircraft industry never again suffered through a period of relative technological stagnation comparable to the 1920s and early 1930s, largely because R&D and procurement funding and domestic and foreign demand for combat aircraft remained at historically high levels throughout the entire Cold War and beyond. Nonetheless, the industry experienced a major downturn following World War II, and later periods of stability and lower rates of technology innovation, when a small number of industry leaders dominated the design and development of mainstream combat aircraft. These periods ended when second-rank,[11] niche, or specialist companies on the market fringes adopted a strategy of high-risk technological innovation in order to break into the top tiers of the market and beat the market leaders—the same pattern that had been estab-

---

[11]*Second-rank* refers to those prime contractors during a specific technology era that enjoyed significantly smaller shares of the combat aircraft market than did the market leaders. However, it is not meant to suggest or imply that such firms were necessarily any less capable or skilled in design and development than the market leaders were.

lished at the end of the biplane era and the beginning of the monoplane revolution.

The following three chapters summarize the industry structure and competition and innovation trends evident in the remaining technology eras as identified at the beginning of Chapter One. They provide a higher-level overview of the remaining technology eras than is presented in this chapter and the preceding chapter on the biplane era and the prop monoplane revolution. Nonetheless, the available evidence seems to confirm the underlying dynamic patterns of competition and innovation that we have reviewed for the period of the 1930s.[12]

---

[12]Chapters Four through Six draw heavily and directly on Mark Lorell and Hugh Levaux, *The Cutting Edge: A Half Century of U.S. Fighter Aircraft R&D*, Santa Monica, Calif.: RAND, MR-939-AF, 1998. Readers wishing greater detail on these later periods should consult this document and other scholarly works cited in the text, footnotes, and Bibliography.

Chapter Four

THE SUBSONIC- AND EARLY SUPERSONIC-JET REVOLUTIONS

On the eve of Pearl Harbor, predicting which U.S. companies would emerge as the new leaders in development of the modern fighter types that had resulted from the monoplane revolution of the mid-1930s was still not obvious. The Lockheed P-38, Bell P-39, Curtiss P-40, Grumman F4F, and Brewster Buffalo were the most modern U.S. Army and Navy fighters in the active inventory when the war started. Yet, with the exception of the P-38—which was available in only very small numbers at the beginning of the war—these fighters were generally outclassed by the leading Japanese and German fighters against which they had to fight. None of these fighters—except for the P-38—remained in production by the later stages of the war.[1]

Some companies—both former leaders and new entrants—ultimately did not fully succeed in the new fighter R&D competition that was launched by the monoplane revolution of the mid-1930s

---

[1]Well into 1943, most USAAF fighter pilots in the Pacific were equipped with P-39s and P-40s; Navy and Marine pilots flew mainly F4Fs and Buffaloes. The Japanese Mitsubishi A6M Zero could easily outclimb and outmaneuver any of these aircraft, had heavier armament (two 20mm cannons), and could cover a much longer range. The only advantages the U.S. aircraft possessed were that they could outrun the Zero in a dive and were better protected with armor plate and self-sealing fuel tanks. As a result, the Japanese essentially retained air superiority in most theaters until the P-38 Lightning, F4U Corsair, and F6F Hellcat began entering service in significant numbers in 1943. See Yoshimura (1996). The Brewster Buffalo ended the war with a particularly poor reputation in the United States. However, recently published research suggests that the basic design was actually quite competitive (Ford, 1996).

and reached its climax during World War II, during its period of refinement (1940–1945). Some would fail completely during the technology revolution wrought by the jet engine after the war, including a leader of the 1920s and 1930s—Curtiss—as well as new entrants during the prop monoplane revolution, such as Brewster and Bell.[2]

These firms withdrew from the combat aircraft market in part because of the precipitous decline in procurement budgets following the end of World War II in August 1945. Nonetheless, in stark contrast to the period following World War I, procurement and particularly R&D budgets rapidly recovered from the postwar reductions. The outbreak of the Korean War in 1950 was followed by a major spike in U.S. procurement and R&D budgets. Although those budgets again declined following the end of the Korean War in 1953, the average peacetime level of military aircraft R&D and procurement budgets remained at a dramatically higher level than was typical before World War II. As shown in Figure 4.1, the overall U.S. defense budget in constant dollars remained at a high level from 1950 through 2000. The exceptions were three large bulges: the Korean War bulge, the Vietnam War bulge, and the Reagan defense-buildup bulge. On the whole, however, the overall demand side remained at historically high levels throughout the Cold War.

The result was that following the shake-out of less-competitive contractors at the end of World War II, R&D and procurement budgets remained at a high enough level through at least the early 1990s to support at least seven credible military combat-aircraft prime contractors at any given time. Thus, competition among contractors remained strong throughout the entire Cold War era.

For our purposes, the most potentially interesting issues to examine during this period involve the structure of the industry, and

---

[2]Although Bell went on to a very successful business building helicopters, Curtiss and Brewster were no longer aerospace prime contractors by the 1950s.

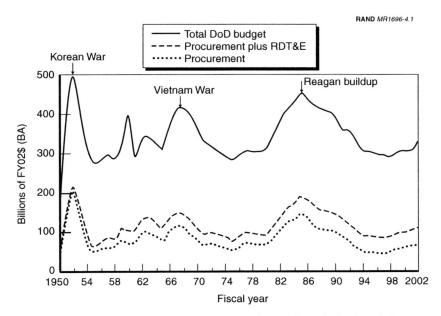

RAND *MR1696-4.1*

Figure 4.1—U.S. Defense Budget, Procurement, and R&D, 1950–2002

particularly the status and market positions of the firms that initiated new periods of higher levels of technology innovation that led to new technology eras. These are the issues that we focus on in this chapter for the subsonic and supersonic revolutions.

THE SUBSONIC-JET ERA, 1945–1953

The Subsonic-Jet Revolution, 1942–1947

By the end of World War II, North American, Republic, Lockheed, Grumman, and Vought had clearly shown the most skill and innovation at exploiting the new monoplane technologies first developed in the early 1930s, emerging as the United States' most successful fighter developers and manufacturers.[3]

Republic (Seversky), Grumman, and Vought had all had significant fighter R&D experience before the war; North American and Lockheed had had little or none. None of these companies, except Grumman, had been important fighter developers until the monoplane revolution of the early 1930s helped break the hold of Curtiss and Boeing on the fighter market. And Grumman had been an early pioneer of key changes that led to the revolution. Curtiss had failed to adapt well to the new technological environment, and Boeing's resources had essentially been diverted to heavy bomber development, especially once the high-priority and technologically demanding B-29 program had gotten under way during the war.[4]

Although it developed excellent designs, U.S. industry had helped win the war primarily by massively outproducing both Germany and Japan, not by developing and applying the world's most innovative cutting-edge aeronautical technologies. By 1943, U.S. government planners had selected a small number of competent, robust military aircraft designs on which to standardize production.[5] The emphasis

---

[3]Lockheed's famous two-engine P-38 played a critical role in winning air superiority after the early stages of the war, and remained in production throughout the conflict. The majority of observers would agree that the most successful conventional Army Air Force fighters of the war were the North American P-51 Mustang and the Republic P-47 Thunderbolt. With a total production run of 15,683, the P-47 was the most heavily produced U.S. fighter of the war and was used with great success in every theater of the war except Alaska. Although it enjoyed a slightly smaller production run of 14,855, the P-51—especially the "D" version—is usually considered the United States' best fighter of the war. Grumman's F6F Hellcat became the Navy's first carrier-based fighter to clearly outclass the Japanese Zero and contributed significantly to turning the war around in the Pacific. The high-performance Vought F4U Corsair is also considered one of the great fighters of the war; it continued to be produced for many years after the war ended.

[4]During the war, Boeing developed and flight-tested an advanced piston fighter prototype with contra-rotating props for the Navy, called the XF8B-1. R&D proceeded slowly, however, as Boeing's resources became ever more heavily committed to development of the B-29 and other bombers. When the war ended, the Navy cancelled the XF8B-1 program, thus grounding the last flying fighter prior to the JSF X-32 technology demonstrator, for which Boeing acted as the prime contractor.

[5]Over three-quarters of total wartime military aircraft production took place from 1943 on. Only 19 models of military aircraft made up nearly 90 percent of that production. Total wartime military aircraft production stood at just under 300,000. See Bright (1978) and Stoff (1993).

was placed on refining these existing designs while maximizing production output. Thus, although U.S. industry produced some of the best operational fighters of the war, the United States had actually fallen even farther behind several other countries in advanced aeronautical technology and innovation during the war, especially Germany and Britain.

In a world of even more rapidly changing technology, the U.S. industry leadership positions newly established during World War II would not necessarily be easy to maintain. Only a decade after the monoplane revolution of the mid-1930s had contributed to the emergence of new U.S. leaders in fighter R&D, another technology revolution was about to take place, centering on jet propulsion and very-high-speed flight. For the most part, U.S. companies in 1945 were not initially well positioned to take leadership roles in the new technologies, most of which had been developed in Germany and the United Kingdom. But in the end, the organizational and structural changes in the industry and government wrought by World War II would help U.S. companies with the right mix of innovation and competition to rapidly meet the challenge and help the United States move toward world leadership in fighter R&D.

The period from 1942 through 1947 can best be characterized as a time of particularly rapid and dramatic technological advancement and change, as developers exploited the enormous increases in potential performance made possible by the jet engine.[6] The Bell P-59, the United States' first operational jet, first flew in 1942 and proved to be a disappointment. Its performance was actually inferior to that of the most advanced prop fighters of the time. Five years later, the North American F-86 made its maiden flight, demonstrating a significant leap in capabilities over the P-59 as well as over advanced prop fighters, particularly in maximum speed and rate of climb, as shown in Table 4.1. It evolved into the most famous and successful fighter of the subsonic-jet era.

---

[6]Early U.S. jet engines were license-produced versions of British-developed engines. The subsonic-jet revolution could be characterized as largely a revolution in propulsion. Until the supersonic-jet revolution, changes in airframe materials, design, and configuration were more modest than those of the monoplane revolution. See Younossi et al. (2002), Appendix B.

Table 4.1

Prop Fighter Versus Subsonic-Jet Fighter Performance

Performance Measure	North American P-51D	Bell P-59A	Lockheed P-80A	North American F-86A
First flight	17 November 1943	1 October 1942	8 January 1944	1 October 1944
Maximum speed (mph)[a]	437	409	558	601
Rate of climb (ft/min)	3,475	NA	4,580	7,470
Service ceiling (ft)	41,900	46,200	45,000	48,000

SOURCE: Data are from Marcelle Size Knaack, *Post–World War II Fighters: 1945–1973*, Washington, D.C.: Office of Air Force History, 1978; and William Green and Gordon Swanborough, *The Complete Book of Fighters*, New York: Smithmark, 1994.

[a]At 25,000 ft for the P-51D, sea level for the P-80A, and 35,000 ft for the P-59A and F-86A.

NA = not available.

Although less than two months separated the first flights of the most famous monoplane prop fighter model (P-51D) and the prototype of the first successful subsonic-jet fighter (P-80), the potential advance in performance was revolutionary. The P-80 prototype, using first-generation immature jet technology, showed about a 25-percent increase in maximum speed and rate of climb over the most-advanced version of the most famous U.S. prop fighter.

Thus, the period from 1942 through 1947 was one of tremendous innovation, new ideas, and wide-ranging experimentation with novel concepts for the U.S. aircraft industry, all of which ultimately led to revolutionary advances in combat aircraft performance. Particularly in the immediate postwar years, it was also an era when relatively new firms as well as established industry leaders had to struggle and fiercely compete to survive in a peacetime world in which the gigantic production orders of World War II no longer existed. Important changes in industry leadership took place during this period, but many of the industry leaders in fighter R&D, which had emerged during World War II, remained competitive. At the same time, relatively new entrants were able to take advantage of rapidly advancing technology to also rise to leadership positions.

This period was thus characterized by continuing robust competition among prime contractors specializing in combat aircraft, as shown in Figure 4.2. Although the numbers of contractors with this specialty declined from the wartime peaks, by 1955 11 prime contractors were still active in this area: Republic, Lockheed, and Northrop concentrated on Air Force fighters; North American and Convair specialized in Air Force fighters and bombers; McDonnell performed well with both Air Force and Navy fighters; three other firms— Grumman, Vought, and Douglas—specialized in Navy fighters; and Boeing and Martin focused on bombers, but also participated in fighter competitions. These contractors made possible the continuation of robust and intense competition in combat aircraft after the war.

The three leading wartime USAAF fighter developers—Lockheed, Republic, and North American—held the initial lead in the immediate postwar Air Force fighter market with their F-80, F-84, and F-86 designs. But jet-fighter technologies were so new and evolving so rapidly that nearly all credible aircraft contractors had a reasonable shot at new fighter R&D work and thus entered the fray. Indeed, at one point in the immediate postwar period, the Air Force was simultaneously funding eight jet-fighter and seven jet-bomber R&D programs by a wide range of contractors. As the Air Force and Navy sought new and innovative R&D proposals in a rapidly changing technology environment, aggressively innovative firms could successfully compete during this period with the established leaders who had much more experience in fighter development (Bright, 1978, p. 11).

For example, the Navy's very first jet-fighter R&D contract went to a virtually unknown company that had been in existence for only three and one-half years and had never developed a Navy fighter or any type of military aircraft that had been purchased in quantity. However, the company had produced an innovative prop fighter

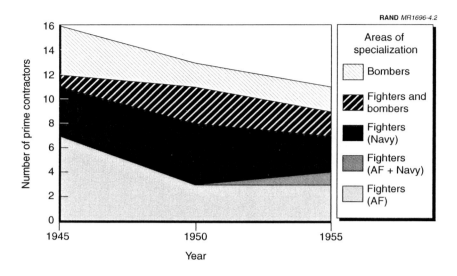

**Figure 4.2—Number of Combat-Aricraft Prime Contractors, 1945–1955.
Even with a decline, a robust, competitive environment is maintained.**

prototype for the USAAF called the XP-67. That company—the McDonnell Aircraft Corporation—received an R&D contract for the Navy's first jet fighter, the FH-1 Phantom, in January 1943. North American, another young—although highly successful—company, which had never developed a Navy fighter, won an R&D contract for a carrier-based jet fighter on New Year's Day in 1945. The Air Force later selected a modified version of North American's Navy jet, designated the FJ-1 Fury, as the basis for the P-86 (later F-86).

North American was one of the dynamic new companies that had succeeded spectacularly with the final generation of prop fighters following the early-1930s monoplane revolution and then had made the transition, with great success, to the jet era. This young, innovative company was one of the firms that recognized early on the great significance of recently captured German research data on advanced aerodynamics.

All early U.S. jet-fighter designs used traditional straight-wing planforms. After studying German research documents, North American engineers concluded early on that, by delaying the onset of compressibility effects, swept-back wings would provide dramatic performance improvement in speed without the need to increase engine thrust. North American began lobbying the Air Force to fund development of this design concept. In November 1945, the Air Force approved North American's proposal to change its XP-86 design, which it had derived from its straight-wing Navy FJ-1 configuration, to a swept-wing planform. First flown in October 1947, the F-86 Sabre became the most successful and most famous U.S. fighter in the Korean conflict during the early 1950s. The F-86 went on to become recognized as the most successful and most famous of the subsonic U.S. fighters.

Subsonic-Jet Technology Refinement, 1947–1953

Thus, an extremely competitive environment, combined with the emergence of jet power and many other new technological opportunities, led to a highly innovative period throughout the five years that we have labeled the "subsonic revolution." From 1947 through the early 1950s, fighter and bomber contractors continued to refine and incrementally improve subsonic fighters. Yet, by the end of the Korean War, the most-advanced subsonic jet fighters had not brought about new large advances in basic performance beyond what had been achieved by the F-86 in 1947. Contractors continuously refined and improved their designs, but it took a new technology revolution to achieve another truly spectacular leap in performance.

We symbolically date the beginning of that revolution from 1953, the year of the first flight of the North American F-100 fighter.

THE SUPERSONIC-JET ERA, 1953–1981

Even more than the subsonic-jet revolution, the supersonic-jet revolution illustrates how U.S. prime contractors, in an intensely competitive environment, often adopted high-risk strategies of tech-nology innovation to win major combat-aircraft development and production contracts. Such strategies were practiced particularly by second-rank contractors seeking to displace existing market leaders.[7]

The remainder of this chapter reviews the period that we have la-belled the "early supersonic jet sub-era." The next chapter examines the other sub-era, "agile supersonic technology."

The Early Supersonic-Jet Revolution, 1953–1962

The increases in speed and altitude capabilities of fighters and bombers escalated even more dramatically during the 1950s, due, at least in part it appears, to a continuation of a highly competitive in-dustry structure in which large numbers of capable industry prime contractors competed for every fighter and bomber contract. Such an environment was fostered and, in fact, made possible by generous government funding and a strong service interest in continued inno-vation. Indeed, the strong upswing in combat aircraft R&D and pro-curement funding stimulated by the outbreak of the Korean War was a critical spur to the competition and innovation underlying the supersonic-jet revolution.

By the early 1950s, large advances in jet-turbine engine power and efficiency, the advent of the afterburner, and resolution of the basic aerodynamic design problems posed by very-high-speed flight, led to an explosion in aircraft speed and altitude capabilities.[8] Compared with first-generation jets, second- and third-generation fighters and bombers became ever faster, higher-flying, heavier, and larger. To il-lustrate the revolutionary advance in performance brought about by the supersonic revolution, Table 4.2 compares some basic perfor-

---

[7]*Second-rank* refers to those prime contractors during a specific technology era that enjoyed significantly smaller shares of the combat aircraft market than did the market leaders. However, it is not meant to suggest or imply that such firms were necessarily any less capable or skilled in design and development than the market leaders were.

[8]For an overview of the history of technology innovation in the aircraft gas-turbine industry and of the innovations that made the supersonic revolution possible, see Younossi et al. (2002), Appendix B.

Table 4.2

Subsonic Versus Supersonic Fighters

Performance Measure	North American F-86F	Convair F-106A	Lockheed YF-12A
First flight	19 March 1952	26 December 1956	July 1962
Maximum speed (mph) [a]	691	1,267	2,275
Rate of climb (ft/min)	6,000	39,800	NA
Service ceiling (ft)	45,000	52,000	80,000

SOURCE: Data are from Marcelle Size Knaack, *Post–World War II Fighters: 1945–1973,* Washington, D.C.: Office of Air Force History, 1978; and William Green and Gordon Swanborough, *The Complete Book of Fighters,* New York: Smithmark, 1994.

[a] F-86F at 35,000 ft; YF-12A at 80,000 ft.

NA = not available.

mance data for the North American F-86F (often considered the premier fighter of the subsonic-jet era) with the Convair General Dynamics[9] F-106A (labeled the "ultimate" fighter of the early supersonic revolution) and the Lockheed YF-12A (an extremely high-speed aircraft tested but never procured as a fighter).

What factors had stimulated the supersonic revolution? Shocked by the advanced state of German aero technology after examining captured documents and programs following the victory in Europe, the U.S. services and U.S. industry adopted a procurement strategy focused on technology innovation rather than sheer numbers. This change in emphasis from the war years helped lead to the tremendous advance represented by the subsonic-jet fighter. This approach was greatly reinforced by a second shock: the unveiling of extremely capable advanced Soviet jet fighters such as the MiG-15 during the Korean War. Generously funded, and faced by intense competition

---

[9] Electric Boat and Canadair merged in 1952, forming General Dynamics (GD). In 1954, GD acquired Convair. However, the main Fort Worth facility was still routinely referred to as Convair until the early 1960s.

from within the industry as well as from the Soviet Union, U.S. industry launched into a new level of innovation during the Korean War, a level never before witnessed in aviation history.

The technological challenges that supersonic flight posed for aerodynamics, materials, and propulsion were daunting. In many respects, they called for far more radical airframe changes than had been dictated by the transition from fast prop fighters to first-generation jets. As contractors began their quest to meet service requirements for the ultimate Mach 3 fighters and bombers, a wide variety of demanding design and other technical challenges had to be addressed, including dramatic new wing shapes and cross sections, novel fuselage-shaping requirements to solve the problem of transonic drag, variable-geometry air inlets, variable-geometry and variable-incidence wings, engine afterburners, manufacturing with titanium and other exotic materials, and a myriad of others. Meeting these challenges contributed dramatically to the escalation in cost, weight, and complexity of fighters and bombers witnessed in the 1950s. None of these technological advances would have been pursued with tenacity without strong service support and generous government funding, as well as a highly competitive industry structure with numerous qualified players.

At the beginning of the 1950s, the new and daunting technical challenges posed by the development of supersonic fighters and bombers helped reduce the relative advantage of experience possessed by industry's leading fighter developers, and once again raised the importance of agile, innovative management and design approaches. Thus, the new technological demands of supersonic flight and weapon system development helped permit innovative new entrants, such as McDonnell and Convair, to be catapulted into leadership positions in fighter development.

After intense competition, a company with little experience or reputation in fighter R&D—Convair (formerly Consolidated Vultee)—initially won the coveted award of developing the ultimate supersonic fighter for the Air Force: the F-102.[10] Why was this task

---

[10]Consolidated Aircraft merged with Vultee Aircraft in March 1943 to become Convair. Consolidated was a leader in bombers, seaplanes, and other large aircraft. In the 1930s, Consolidated developed the most famous seaplane used extensively in

not entrusted to one of the Air Force's leading fighter developers at the time—North American, Republic, or Lockheed? The Air Force recognized that supersonic flight represented a significant leap ahead in fighter design, configuration, and technology. Analysts of the period suggest that Convair had adopted an innovative strategy and had developed skills applicable to supersonic flight that other contractors did not possess. Thus, an inexperienced but innovative company with relevant capabilities could have an advantage over another dominant company with much greater experience in the old technologies.

Recognizing the high degree of technological risk inherent in the F-102 effort, the Air Force in late 1951 divided the program into two stages. The first stage would produce the F-102A as an interim, lower-capability interceptor. The F-102B would be a more advanced version that would appear at a later date as the "Ultimate Interceptor." However, the F-102A program experienced many serious developmental problems and delays. By 1956, the F-102B program became a separate R&D effort for a highly modified variant of the F-102. This new fighter was eventually designated the Convair F-106 Delta Dart.

Both North American and Lockheed were understandably disappointed with Convair's win in the 1951 design competition. Having lost what many considered the most important fighter competition of the early 1950s, both companies feared that without the opportunity to build up more supersonic fighter R&D experience, they were at risk of being forced out of the fighter business. Consequently, both companies continued in-house design studies and wind-tunnel testing in the hopes that the Air Force could still be convinced to support one of their proposals.

World War II, the PBY Catalina. Before the war, the company also concentrated on trainers and a heavy fighter (the P-30). Although less well known than Boeing's two famous wartime bombers (B-17 and B-29), Consolidated's B-24 Liberator was built in larger numbers for U.S. and foreign armed services than was any other single type of U.S. aircraft during World War II. Vultee was not a leading prewar prime contractor. Before the war, Vultee developed a fighter, attack aircraft, and light bombers, which were primarily exported. Consolidated and Vultee produced some experimental fighter prototypes during the war as their only experience in fighter R&D.

Since 1949, North American had worked on its Sabre-45 proposal, a supersonic fighter proposal directly derived from its successful F-86 Sabre design. North American's design efforts also benefited from another Air Force R&D program that was providing considerable insights into supersonic aerodynamic problems: the Air Force X-10/SM-64 Navaho program. As early as 1946, the company had been selected as the prime contractor for this crucial pioneering R&D effort on supersonic flight. Unlike the much slower and more conventional Martin TM-61 Matador and Northrop SM-62 Snark cruise missile programs, and the much shorter-range Boeing Bomarc surface-to-air missile effort, this program sought to develop an unmanned intercontinental Mach 2.75 cruise missile to deliver strategic nuclear weapons over 5,000 miles against the Soviet Union. The X-10/Navaho, with an empty weight of nearly 26,000 lb, was in the same weight class as most contemporary fighters, and thus amounted essentially to a Mach 2+ long-range fighter R&D program. In essence, North American had already been deeply involved in a design and development effort for a supersonic fighter for several years.[11]

The company's efforts finally paid off when North American was able to sell its Sabre-45 proposal to the Air Force as a less expensive supersonic day fighter to complement the all-weather F-102. The Air Force approved development of North American's F-100 Super Sabre in late 1951. In May 1953, North American's F-100 Super Sabre made its first flight, exceeded the speed of sound in a subsequent flight, and later became the first operational jet capable of sustained level supersonic flight (Knaack, 1978, p. 113).

In the world of naval fighter aviation, Grumman had retained its leadership position during the transition period from prop to jet fighters, but a new company—McDonnell—had also been able to es-

---

[11]The first phase of this remarkably ambitious program aimed at developing the X-10 test vehicle for investigating supersonic cruise aerodynamics. North American engaged in general design studies in the late 1940s and launched the specific X-10 design effort in 1950. The X-10 experienced a successful first flight in October 1953, and later achieved speeds of over Mach 1.8. Three X-10s and seven XSM-64 weapon systems were manufactured before the program was cancelled in 1957. The Navaho effort is clearly recognized as contributing significantly to North American's success at winning the XB-70 competition for a Mach 3 strategic bomber in 1957. See Jones (1980, p. 214) and Miller (1983b, p. 84).

tablish itself. Douglas had moved forward into the new fighter technology, but Vought had stumbled. To regain a leadership role, Vought adopted a strategy of innovation to exploit the supersonic revolution. McDonnell adopted a similar strategy and eventually attained a position of such prominence that the company came to lead the entire U.S. industry in fighter development in the 1960s and 1970s. Grumman, meanwhile, seriously faltered for the first time since an earlier technology revolution of the mid-1930s, when Brewster bested its design for the Navy's first monoplane carrier fighter.

The high demand caused by the Korean War was instrumental in promoting the intense competition and high levels of innovation characteristic of the supersonic revolution. During less than two years, between mid-1951 and early 1953, at the height of the Korean War, the Air Force authorized development of a total of six new supersonic fighters. Together becoming known later as the famous "Century Series" fighters, every one of these programs involved intense competition among at least six credible prime contractors, all of which had recent experience in jet-fighter development: Convair, Lockheed, McDonnell, North American, Northrop, and Republic.

Despite their developmental problems, Convair's F-102 and F-106 were procured in large numbers and served as the backbone of the USAF interceptor force. They represented the first attempt to develop a fully integrated and automated fighter interceptor weapon system. Convair's Mach-2 B-58 Hustler became the world's first supersonic bomber and represented a significant leap in aerospace technology. Emulating North American's formula for success on the F-86, the Texas-based firm parlayed captured German delta-wing data into innovative designs, which won it a leading position in both fighters and bombers.

Convair's rise as a technologically innovative fighter and bomber developer contrasted with the beginning of the decline of one of the great historic leaders in fighter R&D: Republic. When the Air Force cancelled Republic's redundant and overly ambitious XF-103 program in September 1957, this famed developer of fighters began a long decline from which it never fully recovered. Republic, which had specialized almost entirely in developing fast, heavy, fighter/attack aircraft, would find it increasingly difficult to diversify to other types of aircraft or to adjust to the radically changed procurement environment for fighters that emerged later in the 1960s.

Lockheed followed its own highly innovative path after its defeat by Convair for the Ultimate Fighter. Lockheed cast its fate with the novel and rather unpopular lightweight fighter concept. But with the failure to garner widespread Air Force support for the lightweight fighter concept as represented by its F-104, Lockheed began to fade as a leading mainstream fighter contractor. However, Lockheed's Skunk Works established itself in the highly specialized niche area of developing unique, high-performance, extremely innovative reconnaissance aircraft. As a far more diversified aircraft company than Republic, Lockheed was thus able to draw on its extensive fighter experience to move into a related area of high-altitude, high-speed reconnaissance aircraft, an area that would provide it with the unique technology capabilities to catapult it into a leadership position years later in fighter R&D.

Northrop, like Lockheed, staked its future in the early 1950s on the lightweight fighter concept. As a result, this Los Angeles–based company, which had always been considered rather eccentric technologically, failed to win a mainstream development contract for a supersonic fighter, until the 1970s, when the lightweight fighter again came into vogue (see Chapter Five). However, Northrop achieved considerable success in directly related areas by developing its N-156 lightweight fighter concept into the T-38 Talon. The T-38 quickly became the standard U.S. Air Force supersonic trainer, later evolving into the very successful and widely exported F-5 fighter series.

The Navy continued to trail the Air Force in fighter R&D during the supersonic era of the 1950s, as it had during the initial period of jet-fighter development in the 1940s. The Navy supported a far smaller overall number of supersonic fighter R&D efforts, and related technology development and demonstration programs, such as cruise missiles and X-planes, which were so important for building the experience and capability base for the success of Air Force programs. Furthermore, the Navy faced particularly difficult technical problems in trying to develop supersonic fighters that could be launched and recovered from the small space available on aircraft carriers. Nonetheless, the Korean War had convinced the Navy that it must support the development of cutting-edge jet-fighter technology. The Navy was determined not to be caught again in a new conflict with lower-performance aircraft, as it had been at the beginning of the Korean conflict.

However, in the particularly challenging circumstances the Navy faced, Grumman—a premier developer of Navy fighters since the 1930s—faltered and temporarily slipped from its leadership position while experimenting with novel technologies. While developing one of the most successful subsonic carrier attack aircraft of the jet era— the A-4 Skyhawk—Douglas gradually withdrew from first-line fighter development. Interestingly, two secondary Navy-oriented contractors—McDonnell and Vought—charged into the breach and ended up developing not only successful new Navy fighters but also two of the most important and most famous supersonic fighters of the 1950s and 1960s, versions of which were eventually procured in large numbers by the Air Force: the McDonnell F-4 Phantom II and the Vought F8U Crusader.

INDUSTRY STRUCTURE DURING THE SUBSONIC-JET ERA AND EARLY SUPERSONIC-JET SUB-ERA

In summary, the 1940s and 1950s witnessed two major revolutions in combat aircraft: the subsonic-jet era and the early supersonic-jet sub-era. The subsonic-jet era was spurred by the huge demand of World War II, the fierce competition of the immediate postwar era for declining procurement budgets, and access to advanced German technologies and design concepts. The supersonic-jet era was spurred on by the shock of confronting advanced Soviet fighters in combat in Korea and fueled by a large spike in procurement and R&D funding for war. Both these eras were characterized by intense competition at the design stages among large numbers of credible contractors for nearly every major fighter and bomber contract. This competition was often continued well into the hardware-development stage. Such competition appears to have contributed materially to the high degree of innovation in design and technology during these technology revolutions, and to the overall success of most fighter R&D efforts.

Figure 4.3 provides an indication of the highly competitive structure of the industry in the 1950s. In 1954, as many as 13 prime contractors, each with sales of at least $120 million or more and 12,000 employees or more, remained credible competitors for combat aircraft development and production contracts. Six of these prime contractors were among the top 100 firms in America, ranked by total sales, with from 46,000 to 72,000 employees. Notice that the smallest of them all in total sales—McDonnell—later emerged as the leading innovator and developer of advanced fighter aircraft during the agile supersonic-jet revolution in the late 1960s and early 1970s. McDonnell engaged in the classical ploy of a latecomer who adopts an aggressive high-risk strategy of technology innovation to take on the industry leaders.

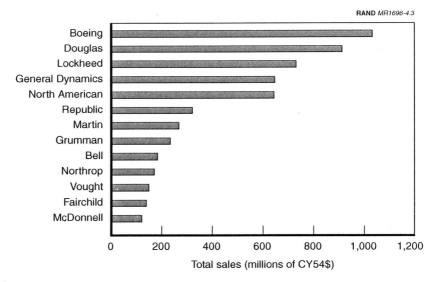

SOURCE: Data are from Donald M. Pattillo, *Pushing the Envelope: The American Aircraft Industry*, Ann Arbor, Michigan: The University of Michigan Press, 2000.
NOTE: Includes commercial and military sales.

Figure 4.3—U.S. Combat-Aircraft Prime Contractors by Total Sales, 1954

The five main Air Force fighter contractors and the four main Navy fighter contractors of the era often crossed over and participated in design competitions sponsored by the other service—and sometimes won those competitions, as did McDonnell for the F-101.[12] Leading contractors were always in danger of losing their position if they did not perform well, and second-rank contractors had a good chance of moving to the forefront if they offered novel technology or designs. The services appear to have carefully nurtured this competition. For example, Grumman was generally viewed as the favored Navy fighter contractor. But when it failed to meet performance requirements with its XF10F and XF11F programs, the Navy awarded its plum contract for a supersonic fighter to McDonnell, possibly in part because of the St. Louis firm's success in developing the supersonic Air Force F-101.

Perhaps even more important, the services sometimes kept full competitions going well into the hardware-development stage—for example, the fly-off between the McDonnell XF-88, the Lockheed XF-90, and the North American XF-93, or the competition between the McDonnell F4H and the Vought F8U-3. Alternatively, the services sometimes supported the development of special proof-testing, flying prototypes before entering into full-scale production, as in the case of the Convair XF-92. Over the years, RAND research has indicated that this type of prototype competition improves the program outcomes of performance, cost, and schedule (Klein et al., 1958; Perry, 1972; Smith et al., 1981; and Lorell, 1989).

SUMMARY

The subsonic and early supersonic revolutions were periods of great technology innovation and experimentation. The armed services and contractors focused on achieving ever-faster and higher-flying combat aircraft. By the end of the 1950s, contracts had been let for the development of fantastic Mach 3+ bombers and fighters.[13] However, it slowly became evident that speeds much beyond the Mach 1 range provided little additional operational utility, particu-

---

[12]McDonnell began the jet era as a Navy contractor.

[13]Good examples are the North American XB-70 bomber program, and the Lockheed YF-12A, the Republic XF-103, and the North American XF-108 fighter programs.

larly given the huge costs and technical challenges posed by the requirements for attaining such speeds. Consequently, all the operational first-generation supersonic fighters developed and procured in
significant quantities by the services remained roughly in the same
performance-capability class as the trailblazing F-100 and F-102/
F-106 fighters. Thus, as far as mainstream operational combat
aircraft, the 1960s witnessed a period of incremental development,
fine-tuning, and refinement of the supersonic fighter technology
innovated in the 1950s.

Chapter Five

THE AGILE SUPERSONIC TECHNOLOGY REVOLUTION

Changes in operational doctrine and other factors caused the 1960s and 1970s to witness shifts in the design emphasis and technology focus for new fighter aircraft. The technological focus on incessantly increasing speed and ceiling, which dominated the 1950s, disappeared in the following decade, replaced by a focus on maneuverability, maintainability, and systems integration. Considered by many as the most capable fourth-generation fighter, the McDonnell-Douglas F-15 nonetheless boasted approximately the same empty weight, ceiling, and top speed as its immediate predecessor, the McDonnell-Douglas F-4. Other highly successful fourth-generation fighters, such as the General Dynamics (now Lockheed) F-16 and McDonnell-Douglas F-18, actually weighed less empty, had lower top speeds, and boasted only modestly higher ceilings than the last second- and third-generation fighters. However, many other performance characteristics, such as agility, turning capability, and specific excess power, were vastly superior in the newer aircraft.

SUPERSONIC TECHNOLOGY REFINEMENT, 1962–1972

The 1960s, a period of reassessment of doctrine and operational requirements and refinement of the supersonic technologies developed in the 1950s, eventually led to the agility revolution. This period might best be broadly characterized as a time of unprecedented intellectual ferment, debate, and disagreement over basic fighter performance and design goals, mission roles, doctrine, and operational concepts. The debate eventually led to a shift in emphasis from heavy, ever-faster, multi-role fighter/attack aircraft, to lighter, more agile, specialized air combat fighters. At the same time, escalating costs led to increasing attempts to reform the weapon system acquisition process.

The intellectual ferment and debate were caused, in part, by dramatic changes in national security doctrine and weapon system procurement policies implemented by the John F. Kennedy administration. Upon entering office, Kennedy's Secretary of Defense, Robert McNamara, began implementing changes in doctrinal emphasis and procurement style that differed fundamentally from those of the 1950s. In strategy and doctrine, the Kennedy administration touted the importance of the "conventional option," emphasizing the ability of the armed forces to fight conventional and limited wars in a nonnuclear environment. McNamara and his "Whiz Kids"[1] at the Defense Department were also determined to impose much greater discipline and rationality on the overall defense planning and budgeting process. The new Defense Department managers were interested particularly in reforming the process by which the services generated new weapon-system performance requirements and developed and procured new hardware (Art, 1968, pp. 30–34).

---

[1]The original "Whiz Kids" were a group of young professionals trained in statistical methods and analysis at the Harvard Business School after World War II broke out, to help the USAAF defeat the Axis Powers. In the late 1940s and the 1950s, RAND pioneered the full development of "Systems Analysis" in the military arena, by developing and applying rigorous mathematical and social scientific methodologies, such as game theory, linear and dynamic programming, network theory, cost analysis, and Monte Carlo methods, to a wide range of defense problems. Before joining the Kennedy administration, McNamara, as president of the Ford Motor Company, had helped introduce modern statistical methods to U.S. corporate management. After becoming secretary of Defense, McNamara was determined to implement similar methods at the Department of Defense, particularly in the areas of weapon system development and budget planning. McNamara recruited a group of young researchers skilled in Systems Analysis, most of whom were from RAND, to implement his reforms. The most important of these were Charles Hitch, the head of RAND's Economics Department, who became the assistant secretary of Defense; and Alain Enthoven, also of RAND, who became a deputy assistant secretary of Defense and helped establish the new Defense Department Office of Systems Analysis. This group became known as McNamara's "Whiz Kids" and provoked considerable controversy and hostility within the traditional armed services leadership. See, for example, Bruce L. R. Smith, *The RAND Corporation: Case Study of a Nonprofit Advisory Corporation,* Cambridge: Harvard University Press, 1969; David Halberstam, *Best and the Brightest,* New York: Random House, 2001; and Fred Kaplan, *The Wizards of Armageddon,* New York: Simon and Schuster, 1983.

McNamara's push to rationalize the procurement process was partly a response to technology and cost trends in the 1950s. The rapidly increasing speed, weight, and technical complexity of first- and second-generation jet fighters and bombers resulted in a dramatic escalation in R&D and procurement costs. As jet-aircraft engine and airframe technology passed out of the early innovation stage and began to mature, each new increment of improvement in speed and altitude capabilities became increasingly challenging technologically—and much more expensive. The growing R&D costs and increasing technological difficulties encountered on such fighter and bomber programs as the F-105, F-106, and B-58 led analysts to question whether even more technologically ambitious programs, such as the Republic F-103 and the North American F-108 and XB-70, were really feasible and cost-effective.[2]

With costs rapidly mounting, defense planners concluded that the large number of full-scale development and prototype technology demonstration programs characteristic of the 1950s could no longer be sustained financially. The Defense Department sought to reduce what it considered to be inefficient duplicative R&D by the services. McNamara cancelled numerous programs and encouraged the services to procure similar or identical aircraft. Indeed, shortly after entering office, McNamara pressured the Air Force to evaluate the Navy McDonnell F4H-1 Phantom II as an interim replacement for the Convair F-106, Republic F-105D, and McDonnell RF-101 Voodoo. After highly successful trials, the Air Force ordered a new version of the Phantom—the F-4C.[3]

---

[2]A counter-argument is that aircraft like the XB-70 were cost-effective because they forced the Soviets to allocate their even-scarcer resources to matching such technologically ambitious programs.

[3]Beginning in June 1957, McDonnell began in-house studies of various Air Force variants of the Phantom II. Never having procured a fighter developed for the Navy, the Air Force initially showed little interest in the Navy proposals. However, flight tests in 1961 and 1962 showed that in several key areas the Phantom generally outperformed—often by a wide margin—the F-106 in the interceptor role, the F-105 in the tactical fighter role, and the RF-101 in the tactical reconnaissance role. Not surprisingly, in March 1962, the Defense Department announced that the Air Force would procure a new version of the Phantom, called the F-110, as its standard tactical fighter. In September 1962, the Defense Department standardized all military aircraft nomenclature. At that time, the F-110 became the F-4C. See Francillon (1990b, pp. 180–181).

The rising unit costs of military aircraft, and the new emphasis on greater commonality of aircraft designs among the services, tended to push procurement trends toward ever smaller numbers of even more-complex and more-expensive fighters designed to offer multi-role and cross-service capabilities.[4] As a result, the 1960s and 1970s witnessed a significant decline in the number of new military manned aircraft R&D programs over the 1950s, by around two-thirds by one accounting of the number of military aircraft designs that were developed and reached first flight during the 1960s. The numbers declined even further in the 1970s.[5]

These trends are clearly reflected in the areas of fighter and bomber R&D. The feverish pace of fighter R&D evident in the 1940s and 1950s slowed considerably during the 1960s. Only two new tactical fighter/bombers were approved for procurement: the McDonnell F-4C for the Air Force and the General Dynamics F-111. The biservice F-111 program, with its success and shortcomings, illustrates the new approach adopted in the 1960s and helps explain why this period was a time of consolidation and refinement rather than of intense and radical technology innovation.

With the cancellation of the F-103, F-107, and F-108 in the late 1950s and the downgrading of the XB-70 bomber to a technology demonstrator project, many contractors anxiously looked forward to three new anticipated R&D programs: one for a future Air Force tactical fighter bomber to replace the F-105, one for a Navy fleet interceptor, and one for a close air support (CAS) combat aircraft. Following the election of President Kennedy, however, Secretary McNamara quickly shattered these expectations. To the great consternation of both contractors and the services, the new Secretary of Defense

---

[4]As discussed later in this chapter, much of the fighter pilot community and various defense reformers rebelled against this concept in the late 1960s, in part because of the relatively poor showing in Vietnam of large, heavy multi-role U.S. fighters, such as the F-4, against smaller, more agile Soviet designs such as the MiG 21. The F-15 and F-16 were subsequently designed as dedicated single-role air combat fighters. But the same cost trends discussed here, combined with a variety of other factors, led the F-16 to evolve toward a heavier multi-role fighter during development, and even the F-15 program eventually produced multi-role attack versions.

[5]See Drezner et al. (1992, pp. 29, 49). According to our data, there were 122 R&D programs for manned military aircraft in the 1950s, compared with 39 such programs in the 1960s and 1970s.

sought to achieve added procurement efficiencies by combining these replacement requirements—minus CAS—into a single aircraft.

Many industry and service officials objected vigorously to this approach, arguing that a single aircraft could not adequately satisfy the performance requirements for both types of missions. Ignoring these criticisms, McNamara forged ahead with his new quest for greater equipment commonality, as reflected in the TFX Request for Proposal (RFP) issued in September 1961. Calling for a 60,000-lb gross take-off weight and low-level supersonic dash capability for the delivery of nuclear and conventional weapons, the TFX requirement asked for a large multi-role fighter-bomber in the same weight class as medium bombers such as the B-57 and B-66 (Knaack, 1978, pp. 223–224).

McNamara began pressuring the Air Force to procure the existing Navy McDonnell F-4 as an interim tactical fighter, pending deployment of the TFX/F-111; expected the Navy to procure the F-111B version as its new fighter; and dramatically cut back on the XB-70 and B-58 bomber programs. As a result, the TFX rapidly emerged as the only major new program on the horizon for both fighter and bomber developers.

In this environment of declining new program starts, nearly all combat aircraft developers entered the TFX competition and fought extremely hard to win the contract. All the leading Air Force fighter developers submitted serious proposals, including General Dynamics, North American, Lockheed, and Republic, as did the leading Navy fighter developers, including Grumman, McDonnell, Douglas, and Chance-Vought. The bomber developers were there, too. Having failed to win either the B-58 or XB-70 strategic bomber competitions in the 1950s, Boeing was determined to win the TFX competition. The Seattle firm, along with many of the other contractors, realized that losing the TFX could lead to an involuntary exit from the combat aircraft industry.

To the surprise of many observers, the Air Force Selection Board and Navy representatives initially selected the Boeing design in January 1962. But the Air Force Council later rejected it. Boeing and the runner-up—General Dynamics, which had teamed with Grumman— then received follow-on study contracts. In June, the Air Force once again selected the Boeing proposal, the Navy refusing to approve this time around. Refined proposals were received in September, and once again the Air Force selected the Boeing design. However, to Boeing's great consternation, McNamara overturned the decision of the uniformed services and gave the contract to General Dynamics (GD) (Knaack, 1978, p. 225).

Congressional testimony suggested that three key factors behind the Secretary's decision were that the GD proposal showed more commonality between the Air Force and Navy versions, that the Texas firm's technical approach was more conservative and credible, and that GD's cost estimates appeared more reliable and believable (Coulam, 1977; Art, 1968).

Winning the F-111 contract assured GD a continuing role as a leader in the development of Air Force fighters and bombers. Air Force adoption of the F-4 Phantom around the same time catapulted McDonnell into the position of the United States' leading manufacturer of tactical fighters. However, the other leading fighter developers seemed to be confronted with grim prospects. Although Grumman had won the lead position for the Navy version of the TFX—the F-111B—the New York firm was clearly subordinate to GD on the program. Far worse were the consequences of the TFX program for the other traditional leading Air Force fighter developers—Republic, North American, and Lockheed—as well as the Navy fighter developers Douglas and Vought.

Failure to win the TFX competition effectively ended the hopes of both Republic and Douglas to remain viable developers of fighter aircraft. Since the 1930s, Republic had specialized almost exclusively in developing large, heavy fighter/attack aircraft for the Air Force. With F-105 production ending in 1964 and GD selected as the developer of the follow-on to the Thunderchief, Republic appeared squeezed out of its specialty market. The company won a reprieve in 1965 when it was purchased by Fairchild Corporation. Hopes for reentry into the fighter market soared briefly when Fairchild-Republic won a contract in 1966 for a new Air Force Vertical Take-Off and Landing (VTOL) fighter to be developed collaboratively with Germany. However, Secretary McNamara cancelled the project in early 1968, once again leaving Republic with no aircraft contracts (Stoff, 1990, pp. 166–167).

As a result of McNamara's policies and GD's victory in the TFX competition, Douglas found itself in a similar position to Republic's with regard to fighter aircraft. In July 1960, Douglas had won a hard-fought competition to develop the Navy's ultimate stand-off air defense fighter, the F6D-1 Missileer. Envisioned to be little more than a long-endurance subsonic missile-launch platform, the Missileer was intended to loiter for hours out in front of the fleet and to launch the Bendix-Grumman XAAM-N-10 Eagle long-range missile at enemy bombers more than 150 miles away. McNamara cancelled this program in April 1961, however, after folding the Missileer mission into the new TFX requirement. As a result, Douglas' survival became almost entirely dependent on its commercial aircraft sales. However, problems with both the DC-8 and DC-9 airliners led to a financial crisis in 1965. The next year, McDonnell bought out the ailing Douglas Corporation and made it a division of the St. Louis–based company. The Douglas division continued to design airliners, but this famous developer of the legendary carrier aircraft that won the Battle of Midway never again developed a Navy fighter or attack aircraft (Bright, 1978, pp. 192–196).[6]

North American, Lockheed, and Northrop found themselves with no prospects for a new first-line fighter program after the TFX decision, but they had other work to keep them busy. North American had increasingly specialized in space platforms and vehicles, in high-speed test aircraft such as the X-15, and in supersonic bombers such as the XB-70 and later B-1A. Lockheed moved ahead vigorously in space and in military and commercial transports. It specialized in high-speed reconnaissance aircraft, including the spectacular Mach 3 SR-71, a version of which the Air Force briefly considered for procurement as the YF-12 fighter/interceptor. Northrop focused heavily on its highly successful lightweight export fighter, the F-5 Freedom Fighter, and the T-38 jet trainer on which it was based.

After the TFX decision, some hope lingered among these traditional Air Force fighter contractors, as well as with Republic, that the Air

---

[6]Douglas SBD Dauntless dive bombers played a central role in sinking four Japanese aircraft carriers at the decisive Battle of Midway in June 1942. They remained the most important carrier-based Navy attack aircraft of the war. Their creator, Ed Heineman, went on to design one of the most famous U.S. carrier-based attack aircraft of the jet era, the Douglas A-4 Skyhawk.

Force requirement for a CAS aircraft might lead to a new fighter/attack aircraft program. As the war in Vietnam began to heat up, many in the Air Force supported procurement of a version of the F-5; others called for a specialized counterinsurgency (COIN) aircraft. To the considerable consternation of the traditional Air Force contractors and many in the Air Force, McNamara once again pushed for greater service commonality by pressuring the Air Force to procure a version of the Navy Vought A-7 attack aircraft, which itself was a development of the Navy Vought F-8 Crusader. In early 1966, the Air Force agreed to procure an upgraded version of the A-7, ending once and for all the hopes of the traditional Air Force fighter contractors for a new program (Gunston, 1974, pp. 234–242).

Thus, by the mid-1960s, McNamara's push for greater service equipment commonality and the development of multi-role fighters had produced a grim outlook for many traditional fighter developers. It appeared that all anticipated fighter and attack aircraft requirements for the Air Force and Navy would be filled by the TFX or by versions of existing aircraft. But increasing technical problems, cost growth, and schedule slippage on the TFX program, combined with growing Air Force and Navy dissatisfaction with anticipated TFX performance limitations in aerial combat, led to a dramatic turnaround of this situation in the late 1960s.

The existence of second-rank but credible prime contractors that were determined to use innovative technology and concepts to supplant the industry leaders led to a continuation of fierce competition. In the end, new R&D efforts were launched that led to some of the most successful and capable conventional jet fighters ever developed by U.S. industry.

THE AGILE SUPERSONIC-JET REVOLUTION, 1972–1974

The Air-Superiority Fighter Requirement

The late 1960s and the 1970s witnessed the development of two new Air Force fighters—the F-15 and F-16—and two new Navy fighters—the F-14 and F/A-18—which would become the mainstays of U.S. tactical fighter forces for the remainder of the century. The two Air Force fighters and the F/A-18 in particular represent a substantial change from many of the trends evident in previous fighter-modernization decisions. The F-15 was the first Air Force fighter since the North American F-86 was developed in the late 1940s that was optimized for maneuverability and agility for dogfights with enemy fighters. In an even more dramatic departure from recent past experience, the F-16 and F-18 programs attempted to reverse the trends toward heavier, more complex, and more costly fighters.

These changes did not come easily. They resulted from a long, arduous, and turbulent process during which various schools of thought on fighter doctrine and design, teamed with prime contractors hungry for new programs, vied for influence. What were often vitriolic debates ended in the design and development of several of the world's most capable fighters.

As early as 1964, a consensus began to emerge within the Air Force that a new tactical fighter was needed. In part, this consensus reflected Air Force dissatisfaction with the TFX program and McNamara's policy of fighter commonality among the services. As serious developmental problems emerged on the TFX program, indicating that the F-111 would not be able to meet all of its multi-role, multi-service performance requirements, various influential elements within the Air Force increasingly voiced the desire for a tactical fighter developed *by* and *for* the Air Force (Gentry, 1976, pp. 9–10).

As the new Air Force fighter concept dubbed the F-X evolved toward an aircraft similar in weight and size to the increasingly controversial F-111, projected R&D costs skyrocketed and opposition within the Air Force mounted. One group of dissenters, later known as the "Fighter Mafia," led by John Boyd, Pierre Sprey, and others, began arguing with considerable effect against such a fighter within the Air Force and the Department of Defense. This group advocated procurement of a much lighter, highly maneuverable dogfighter optimized for close-in air combat.[7]

---

[7]Other leaders of the Fighter Mafia included Everest Riccioni, an experienced F-100C pilot; Charles ("Chuck") Myers, a former test pilot and Navy fighter pilot who worked for Lockheed on the development of the lightweight F-104; John Chupruns at Wright-Patterson AFB; Richard Willis at Nellis AFB; and Al Price at the Air Force Academy. The account presented here draws on a variety of open sources, as well as on interviews conducted by Mark Lorell with Boyd, 8 October 1980; Christie, 19 September 1980; Myers, 24 September 1980; and Sprey, 19 September 1980.

Debate continued on with no action being taken until the revelation of new Soviet fighters galvanized opinion in the Office of the Secretary of Defense (OSD) and the Air Force around the Fighter Mafia's air-superiority concept. In July 1967, at an air show at the Domodedovo airfield near Moscow, the Soviet air force revealed two new highly capable fighters: the MiG-25 Foxbat and the MiG-23 Flogger. Many officials in the Defense Department believed that these new fighters, particularly the MiG-25, would be difficult for the F-4 or other existing U.S. tactical fighters to counter. This revelation reinforced the arguments for a specialized highly maneuverable air-superiority fighter uncompromised by multi-role air-to-ground capabilities.[8]

The F-X and VFX Competitions

In response to these and other factors, the Air Force sent out an RFP in August to seven contractors for a new round of design studies. In December 1967, the Air Force awarded study contracts to the two winning firms: McDonnell-Douglas and General Dynamics. Three other historic Air Force fighter R&D leaders—North American, Lockheed, and Fairchild-Republic—as well as Grumman, also took part in the design study, using their own corporate funds. Although debate continued within the Air Force over design configuration, weight, and multi-role capabilities for the F-X, most Air Force officials now supported an air-superiority fighter and strongly opposed compromising the capabilities of the future F-X by requiring it to fulfill carrier-based Navy or ground-attack missions.

Insurmountable opposition in the Navy to continuing the F-111B finally emerged in response to the same event that crystallized Air Force support for an F-X optimized for air superiority: the revelation of new Soviet fighters at the Moscow Air Show in July 1967. The existence of new-generation Russian fighters, combined with the re-

---

[8]Ironically, neither of the two new Soviet fighters proved to be outstanding dog-fighters, particularly the MiG-25. It allegedly had been developed to counter the Mach 3 XB-70 strategic bomber. Nevertheless, the F-4 did not have the altitude and speed capabilities to deal effectively with the MiG-25.

newed appreciation for the importance of maneuverability and dog-fighting gained from air combat experience over Vietnam, led the Navy to argue convincingly that a specialized Navy fighter optimized for carrier-based fleet air defense was needed. The Navy soon awarded a contract to Grumman for a study evaluating the F-111B capabilities in combat against the new Soviet fighters. In October, Grumman reported that the F-111B would not be able to cope with the new Russian fighters in a dogfight. More important, Grumman submitted an unsolicited design proposal, based on company design studies under way since 1966, for a totally new fighter that could meet the Navy's fleet air defense needs.[9] Shortly thereafter, two other historic Navy fighter developers—LTV (Vought)[10] and McDonnell-Douglas—also submitted design proposals, as did a sea-soned Air Force fighter developer, North American–Rockwell, to what became known as the VFX competition.[11] All these companies, with the exception of LTV, were also active participants in the Air Force F-X design studies. At around the same time, the Navy informed General Dynamics that the F-111B did not meet its requirements and initiated a new study of alternatives.

By fall 1968, Air Force consensus had essentially been achieved on procurement of a highly agile, relatively lightweight fighter optimized for maneuvering air combat. On 30 September 1968, the Air Force sent out a new F-X RFP, based on what was now called the Blue Bird concept, to eight prime contractors. Only four companies responded with serious proposals. Not surprisingly, these were General Dynamics, North American, and Fairchild-Republic—the three his-torical Air Force fighter developers—and McDonnell-Douglas—the emerging U.S. industry leader in fighter R&D. After eliminating General Dynamics—the current industry leader—from the competi-tion, the Air Force awarded contracts for a 6-month project-definition phase to the remaining three contractors on 30 December 1968. Apparently confirming service displeasure with the entire TFX

---

[9]However, Grumman proposed retention of a swing-wing design and many F-111B systems, such as the engines.

[10]In 1961, Chance Vought merged with other companies to form Ling-Temco-Vought, later called LTV. However, aerospace industry observers often continued to refer to LTV as Vought.

[11]In 1967, North American merged with Rockwell Standard to become North American–Rockwell.

affair, the Navy eliminated General Dynamics also from the VFX competition this same month, along with LTV and North American, leaving Grumman and McDonnell-Douglas as finalists.

The VFX competition concluded rapidly. In mid-January 1969, the Navy selected Grumman to develop the VFX, later designated the F-14A Tomcat. The F-X competition took somewhat longer to resolve. In June 1969, McDonnell-Douglas, North American, and Fairchild-Republic submitted their final design proposals for the F-X, now designated the F-15. After six months of extensive evaluations by the Air Force and OSD, the Secretary of the Air Force, on 23 December 1969, announced the selection of McDonnell-Douglas to develop the F-15. Unlike the F-111 contest, no significant disagreements emerged within the government regarding selection of a winner. Nearly all published accounts agree that the McDonnell-Douglas design submission won on technical merit.

On the whole, the F-15 and F-14 fighters proved to be successful, although the Tomcat R&D program experienced considerable controversy in the early 1970s because of high costs and other factors. First delivered to the Air Force in November 1974, the F-15 Eagle rapidly became viewed as the premier air-superiority fighter in the Air Force inventory. In early 1984, the Air Force selected an extensively modified version called the F-15E Strike Eagle for the all-weather deep-attack mission to complement the aging F-111. By the mid-1990s, well over two decades after the F-15's initial entry into service, most observers still considered the Eagle to be the most capable air-superiority fighter in the world. Benefiting from a major upgrade program in the 1990s, the F-14 also continued on in Navy service and remained the world's leading carrier-based fighter. The F-14 program confirmed Grumman's position as the leader for more than four decades in Navy fighter R&D; the F-15 effort indisputably established McDonnell-Douglas as the United States' foremost developer of USAF fighter aircraft.

The Lightweight Fighter Competition

Despite the great success eventually enjoyed by the F-14 and F-15, concerns continued to mount during the R&D programs for these fighters that the unchecked growth in costs for fighter R&D and procurement could not be sustained. Many observers believed that growing costs would inevitably lead to dramatic cuts in planned pro-curement numbers, which, in turn, would result in a dangerous de-cline in overall force-structure size and capabilities. Some Defense Department officials and several contractors began advocating de-velopment of cheaper, lightweight, less-capable fighters that could be procured in larger numbers. Combined with the F-14 and F-15, these fighters would produce a larger force structure composed of a "high-low" mix of capabilities. At the same time, the Fighter Mafia led by Boyd and Sprey, which had always argued that the F-14 and F-15 "Blue Birds" were too large and complex, continued to argue ef-fectively for procurement of cheaper lightweight fighters.[12]

Throughout the first half of 1971, Deputy Secretary of Defense David Packard and other OSD officials became increasingly convinced of the potential benefits of funding a low-cost program for the compet-itive development and fly-off of lightweight fighter prototypes. Such a program not only would provide a candidate lightweight fighter prototype to supplement the F-14 and F-15 if desirable but also could serve as a means of evaluating a variety of proposed acquisition reforms, such as competitive prototyping and performance-based requirements. In January 1972, RFPs for a lightweight fighter proto-type were sent out to nine contractors. The five companies that had been involved in earlier lightweight fighter design studies responded: Boeing, GD, Northrop, LTV, and Lockheed. Although there is some dispute in the open literature over the ranking of the designs sub-mitted by these companies after government officials evaluated them technically, several sources suggest that the designs developed by three firms—Boeing, GD, and Northrop—were considered clearly superior and roughly comparable. On 13 April 1972, the government awarded contracts to GD and Northrop to develop their prototype lightweight fighters for a fly-off competition.

The outcome of the design competition was somewhat surprising, given both Northrop's and Lockheed's advocacy of the lightweight

---

[12]However, Boyd and most of the rest of the Fighter Mafia did not accept the as-sumption that lighter and simpler meant less capable. They argued that complicated, expensive modern fighters did not work well in real combat situations and had poor reliability and maintenance records. Larger numbers of simpler, more agile, more ro-bust, and more reliable fighters, they argued, would actually provide greater overall combat capability for the total force structure.

fighter concept since the early 1950s. The competition pitted one of the leaders of the 1960s that stressed large, heavy fighters—GD—against a more unorthodox second-rank prime contractor—Northrop. However, Lockheed's lightweight fighter submission was seen by some as a rehash of earlier designs ultimately derivative of the F-104 lightweight fighter so unpopular with the Air Force in the 1950s. Furthermore, both GD and Northrop had been working closely with the Fighter Mafia, conducting design studies for a lightweight fighter since the earliest days of the F-X program. GD drew heavily on these years of design studies, as well as on the extensive experience it had gained developing the F-111 and its earlier fighters.

GD's Model 401 design presented no radically new technologies or design concepts. However, it cleverly brought together for the first time a variety of cutting-edge technologies and concepts, including variable camber, blended-body configuration, and a fly-by-wire flight control system to optimize maneuverability while controlling cost. GD's Model 401 had many traits in common with Northrop's P600 design proposal and earlier Northrop lightweight fighter design concepts (Anderson, 1976).[13]

Both lightweight fighter prototypes first flew in 1974. Throughout the last half of the year, military and civilian test pilots flew the GD and Northrop prototypes—now designated YF-16 and YF-17, respectively—in an intensely competitive fly-off.

AGILE SUPERSONIC FIGHTER TECHNOLOGY REFINEMENT, 1974–1981

In January 1975, the Secretary of the Air Force announced that GD's YF-16 had been selected for full-scale development. The product of a successful full-scale development program, the F-16 Fighting Falcon went on to become the most numerous fighter in the Air Force inventory and one of the most widely exported fighters of the past

---

[13]Also in 1970, Northrop and Fairchild-Republic had won the Defense Department's A-X competition to develop prototypes of a relatively simple, low-cost attack aircraft for a competitive fly-off. In January 1973, the Defense Department selected Republic's A-10 prototype over Northrop's A-9 for full-scale development.

several decades. However, the F-16 quickly evolved away from the early lightweight fighter concept as envisioned by the Fighter Mafia in the 1960s, developing into a much heavier, much more capable multi-role fighter-bomber.[14]

In 1975, most observers assumed that, in accordance with the wishes of Congress, the Navy would procure a "navalized" version of the YF-16 to supplement the F-14. Yet, the Navy was unhappy with the YF-16 as selected by the Air Force and with the YF-17. Both aircraft clearly had to be modified considerably in order to be made suitable for use aboard aircraft carriers. Furthermore, the Navy wanted an attack fighter, not a lightweight dogfighter, in part because it wanted to reserve the fleet air defense mission for the F-14.

Both lightweight fighter contractors teamed with traditional Navy fighter developers to design navalized versions: GD with LTV, and Northrop with McDonnell-Douglas. In May, the Navy announced the selection of the Northrop/McDonnell-Douglas team. The teaming arrangement gave leadership to McDonnell-Douglas, as an experienced Navy fighter developer, on Navy variants, and Northrop on any land-based designs. Under the terms of the teaming arrangement, McDonnell-Douglas engineers significantly modified and redesigned the YF-17 prototype into a virtually new strike/attack naval fighter. In recognition of this fact, the aircraft was eventually designated the McDonnell-Douglas/Northrop F/A-18 Hornet.[15] The Hornet became the standard carrier fighter/attack aircraft for the Navy. In the 1990s, McDonnell-Douglas radically modified the Hornet into a new, more capable version called the F/A-18E/F.

---

[14]It has been claimed that the F-16 gained a pound of weight for every day that passed since its first flight. The early Block 5, 10, and 15 versions are close to the original Fighter Mafia concept of an austere, daylight dogfighter. The Block 25 and 30 versions were essentially developed as replacements for the multi-role F-4 fighter/attack aircraft, and were equipped for long-range, radar-guided missile capability. The Block 40 has an enhanced air-to-ground capability, which includes Low-Altitude Navigation and Targeting Infrared System for Night (LANTIRN) and Maverick options. The most recent and highly capable Block 50 and higher versions are versatile world-class multi-role fighter-bombers, some equipped with active phased-array radar and conformal fuel tanks for extended ranges.

[15]According to one McDonnell-Douglas engineer quoted in Orr (1991, pp. 51–52), "The F/A-18 looks like the YF-17, but it is a brand new plane, aerodynamically, structurally, in all ways. It's a brand new airplane from the ground up. . . ."

INDUSTRY STRUCTURE AND COMPETITION DURING THE 1960s AND 1970s

During the 1960s and 1970s, several firms drifted away from the combat aircraft market, essentially exiting the industry as a result of the dramatic decline in the number of new programs since the 1950s. Nonetheless, as shown in Figure 5.1, a significant number of prime contractors remained in the market, guaranteeing the continuation of robust competition. In 1965, 11 prime contractors with combat aircraft specializations—the same number as in 1955—continued to compete. Ten years later, eight prime contractors were still in competition, although several of them had clearly become second-rank contractors. And even the more marginalized among the prime contractors at this time, such as Republic, vigorously competed for major combat-aircraft contracts and could not be ignored.

During the 1960s and 1970s, many of the historical leaders in fighter R&D continued to excel. McDonnell-Douglas raised itself to a po-

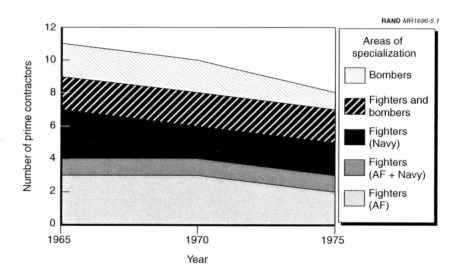

Figure 5.1—Number of Combat-Aircraft Prime Contractors, 1965–1975.
Despite consolidation, competition remains high.

sition of world leadership in tactical fighter R&D through the enormous success of the F-4 Phantom II in both the Navy and Air Force inventories, followed by victory in both the Air Force F-15 and the Navy F-18 competitions (the latter with Northrop), as well as the AV-8B Harrier.[16] General Dynamics (formerly Convair) remained a prominent Air Force developer by winning the F-16 R&D contract, as well as the F-111 fighter-bomber. Grumman maintained its dominant position in naval tactical fighters by working on the F-111B development program and by developing the F-14. As Figure 5.2 demonstrates, nine large prime contractors capable of credibly competing for military aircraft R&D and production contracts were active in 1967, on the eve of the agility revolution. Of these, seven were among the top-100 largest U.S. corporations by total sales.[17]

However, at least three prominent leaders from the 1940s and 1950s were shut out of the mainstream fighter market during this period. Republic, North American, and Lockheed failed to win major fighter contracts. They appeared to have permanently lost their historical positions as important Air Force fighter developers. On the Navy side, the number of dedicated fighter developers shrank to one: Grumman.[18] Douglas had already effectively withdrawn from the fighter market well before the merger with McDonnell. After its success winning the A-7 development contract, Vought, now Ling-Temco-Vought (LTV), failed to garner new fighter R&D programs.

---

[16]A development of the British Aerospace (BAE) Harrier, formerly the Hawker Siddeley Kestrel.

[17]Ryan is included in Figure 5.1 but is not shown in Figure 5.2. By the 1950s, Ryan had essentially exited the mainstream combat aircraft market as a prime contractor. However, it continued to develop and fly Unmanned Air Vehicles (UAVs) and prototype VTOL test aircraft—including the X-13 Vertijet, the VZ-3RY Vertiplane, and the XV-5A/B Vertifan—well into the 1960s. The Vertifan was flight-tested through 1965. Teledyne acquired Ryan in 1968. As a subsidiary of Teledyne, Ryan remained in the aerospace business but ended its role as a prime contractor for manned aircraft. By the mid-1990s, Ryan once again was active in the market as a prime contractor developing large UAVs. In 1998, its highly successful high-altitude long-endurance (HALE) UAV, called RQ-4A Global Hawk, made its first flight. In 1999, Northrop Grumman bought Ryan from Teledyne. The Ryan division continues developing new versions of the Global Hawk UAV, a large aircraft with a wingspan of over 100 ft and a take-off weight in excess of 25,000 lb.

[18]McDonnell-Douglas, of course, remained a leading developer of Navy fighter and other combat aircraft, but it became increasingly involved in the development of fighters for the Air Force.

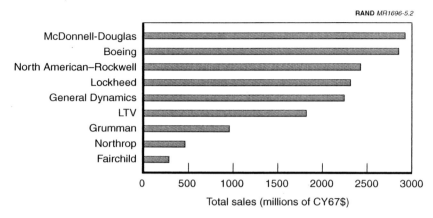

SOURCE: Data are from Donald M. Pattillo, *Pushing the Envelope: The American Aircraft Industry*, Ann Arbor, Michigan: The University of Michigan Press, 2000.
NOTE: Includes commercial and non-aerospace sales.

Figure 5.2—Leading Combat-Aircraft Prime Contractors, 1967

Despite the effective decline in the number of contractors active in fighter-development programs, and despite Secretary of Defense McNamara's emphasis on a systems-analysis approach to design competitions, the 1960s and 1970s still witnessed widespread and intense competition and prototyping not unlike that which charac-terized earlier periods. Indeed, at the concept-definition and design stages, the competition was probably as great during the 1960s and 1970s as during the 1950s. Virtually every major prime contractor submitted credible proposals in nearly every military aircraft effort during this period. With the relative decline of service specialization among contractors, the number of credible entrants in a competition often increased over what was typical earlier. Even a company like Boeing, which specialized in transports and subsonic bombers, be-came a very serious and credible contender in fighter competitions, at least at the design stage, as shown in Table 5.1.[19] Most indepen-dent observers also considered North American–Rockwell, Fairchild-

---

[19]Various accounts claim that Boeing was the initial winner in the TFX design com-petition. Boeing is reported by some published sources as having presented a pro-posal considered roughly comparable to those provided by GD and Northrop on the

Table 5.1

Important Role of Second-Rank Competitors in Fighter/Attack Aircraft R&D, 1960s to 1980s

Second-Rank Fighter Prime Contractor	Contractor Competition Status and Program		
	Major Entrant	Finalist	Winner
Boeing	A-6, ATF (F-22)	F-111, F-16	
Fairchild-Republic	F-111	F-15	A-10
North American–Rockwell	A-7, F-14, ATF	F-15	X-31
LTV	A-6, F-111, F-14, F-5E, F-16, F-18		A-7

Republic, and LTV to be very serious competitors throughout this period, even though they never won a fighter design competition.[20]

Despite the infamous "paper competitions" advanced by McNamara's Whiz Kids in the Defense Department, which contributed to the early problems experienced on the TFX (F-111) and C-X (C-5A) R&D programs, the 1960s and 1970s witnessed major new initiatives in competitive prototyping unmatched by anything seen since the late 1940s and early 1950s. The most obvious examples are the fly-offs between the GD YF-16 and Northrop YF-17, as well as the Northrop A-9 and Republic A-10.

SUMMARY

In short, the period from the early supersonic-jet revolution through the agile supersonic-jet revolution exhibited uninterrupted and

---

lightweight fighter design competition for the Air Force. The Seattle firm also reportedly did well on the F-X competition.

[20]Published accounts allege that Republic came in a close second on the F-X (F-15) design competition and submitted competitive proposals on the lightweight fighter program and other competitions. North American was a finalist on the F-X and is claimed to have been a serious contender on the F-14 program. Some accounts allege that LTV was a serious contender on the F-14, F-16, F/A-18, and F-5E programs.

robust competition among eight or more credible contractors for the small number of new tactical combat aircraft and bomber programs. By the late 1970s, two or three firms had become the dominant contractors for combat aircraft. Nonetheless, vigorous second-rank contractors continued to compete fiercely, some of them still willing and able to take major risks with new technology and other innovations to regain leadership roles.

Chapter Six

THE STEALTH REVOLUTION

The dawn of the stealth era is an excellent example of the dynamic of second-rank contractors taking greater technological risks and emphasizing innovation in order to unseat the established industry leaders. As during the monoplane revolution and subsequent technology eras, second-rank prime contractors often led the way in new-technology innovation in the course of intense competition with those leading prime contractors that dominated the market for conventional-technology combat aircraft.

INDUSTRY LEADERS IN THE STEALTH REVOLUTION

The stealth era, which got fully under way in the mid-1970s, behind a wall of strict secrecy, ushered in a new era of rapid technology change. Armed with precision-guided munitions, the new generation of U.S. stealthy combat aircraft dramatically increased the potential combat effectiveness of air power. Developed and applied primarily by U.S. contractors, stealth technology guaranteed that U.S. developers of military aircraft remained in an unquestionable position of world leadership. The stealth revolution transformed military aircraft airframe and avionics design and development, and led to major changes in U.S. industry leadership in fighter R&D.

The key technologies for achieving low-radar-cross-section (RCS) manned combat aircraft included the development of advanced composite materials and fabrication processes for large load-bearing aircraft structures and engine structures; advanced radar-absorbing materials (RAM) and application processes; measurement devices and methodologies for accurately measuring RCS; significantly improved computers and advanced computer-assisted design (CAD) processes to assist in shaping aircraft structure; and advanced fly-by-wire (FBW) computer-controlled electronic flight-control systems to provide flight stability for aerodynamically unstable low-RCS designs (Pace 1992, pp. 219–220). Later, engineers also had to develop fire-control radars and other avionics with less-detectable emissions, such as low-probability-of-intercept (LPI) radar. Low-observable (LO) engine development was also undertaken. Most of these technologies had been under development in the 1970s or earlier for a variety of applications, but Lockheed and Northrop first brought them all together in an operationally effective way for stealth combat aircraft.

The stealth era exhibits several broad characteristics in common with the monoplane, subsonic-jet, and supersonic-jet eras. Like these earlier periods of fighter R&D, the stealth era witnessed a significant amount of technological change in basic airframe/air vehicle development, which had the effect of leveling the playing field for several aerospace prime contractors.

ORIGINS OF THE STEALTH REVOLUTION

On the eve of the stealth revolution in the 1970s, up to eight robust prime contractors still remained credible competitors for fighter/attack aircraft contracts, as shown in Figure 6.1. At this time, McDonnell-Douglas, with its F-4, F-15, F-18, and Harrier programs, could be viewed as the preeminent developer of Air Force, Navy, and Marine fighter/attack aircraft. General Dynamics and Grumman maintained their strong leadership roles in Air Force and Navy fighters and fighter-bombers. North American was transitioning from a focus on supersonic fighters to specialization in supersonic bombers and spacecraft. Boeing was the dominant supplier of subsonic heavy bombers. Republic, which had specialized in heavy Air Force fighter/attack aircraft, soldiered on with its A-10 attack aircraft. Focusing on Navy fighters, Vought (Ling-Temco-Vought) had slipped to second-rank status. Having lost their leadership positions in the 1950s in mainstream fighter, fighter/attack, and bomber development, Lockheed and Northrop continued to thrive in niche specialty-aircraft areas.

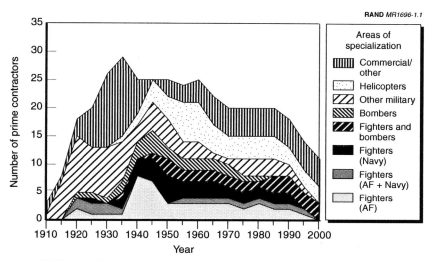

NOTE: In addition to the larger prime contractors specializing in larger commercial and military fixed-wing aircraft, this figure includes most of the smaller leading commercial prime contractors specializing in general-aviation aircraft, business aircraft, and rotary-wing aircraft

Figure 6.1—Number of Combat-Aircraft Prime Contractors, 1975–1990. A stable number ensures robust competition for the stealth revolution.

The stealth revolution was an era of major technological innovation and change that enhanced opportunities for new entries into specialized areas among the prime contractors. In the 1940s and 1950s, the turbo-jet engine revolution permitted companies such as McDonnell, which was founded in 1939 and had no major development contracts in World War II, to come out of nowhere and become a leading developer of both Navy and Air Force jet fighters. Leading fighter developers of the 1930s and 1940s, such as Bell and Curtiss, failed to successfully accomplish the transition to jets. Boeing, the dominant heavy-bomber developer of World War II, slipped behind North American and Convair in the mid-1950s, in part because of its relative lack of experience in the rapidly advancing technologies associated with supersonic flight. Likewise, the stealth revolution permitted two companies—Northrop and Lockheed—which had specialized in niche combat-aircraft areas and had not been the leading mainstream fighter and bomber developers in the 1960s and 1970s, to take a clear leadership role in stealth combat aircraft in the 1980s and 1990s. Conversely, the dominant mainstream fighter and bomber developers during the 1960s and 1970s—McDonnell-Douglas, General Dynamics, Grumman, and Rockwell—which had built their leadership based on their substantial expertise in conventional supersonic combat-aircraft development, ended up losing most of the competitions for the new stealth combat platforms.

Good fortune related to firm-specific capabilities acquired from its niche specialties in the 1950s and 1960s appears, in part, to have helped Lockheed arrive at its strong position as a leader in stealth. For its part, Northrop appears to have made a strategic corporate decision as far back as the 1960s to concentrate on stealth technologies as one element of a strategy to break out of its second-rank position among combat aircraft contractors by increasing its unique firm-specific capabilities.[1]

The F-104, Lockheed's last fighter procured by the Air Force before the stealth era, began development in the early 1950s. After this point, Lockheed continued to compete for numerous mainstream fighter and bomber programs, but it failed to win them. The company increasingly specialized in large aircraft (military and commercial transports, and maritime patrol aircraft), as well as top-secret, highly specialized reconnaissance aircraft developed at its famous Skunk Works facility in Burbank, California.

Aircraft designed for covert strategic reconnaissance missions are intended, of course, not to be detected. Launching development of their U-2 reconnaissance aircraft in 1954, Lockheed designers sought to ensure survivability and avoid detection by making the aircraft small and providing it with very-high-altitude capabilities. Some studies were conducted on reducing the U-2's radar cross section, but they did not meet with great success. However, the follow-on to

---

[1]Most of the details about the history of stealth R&D are still sketchy or remain classified. The account presented here has been pieced together from a variety of open sources, which may not be accurate and often tend to be incomplete. A full and accurate account of this period will have to await the declassification of substantially more information.

the U-2 was the first aircraft designed from its inception to reduce RCS.

Eventually known as the SR-71 Blackbird, this remarkable aircraft was approximately the same size as the Convair B-58 medium bomber, flew at Mach 3+ at altitudes over 80,000 ft, but had the RCS of a small private aircraft (Rich and Janos, 1994, pp. 23–24). By the mid-1960s, a full-scale model of the SR-71 was being tested on an RCS test range. To achieve the first stealthy military aircraft, Lockheed employed radar-absorbing materials for structural edges and radar-absorbing coatings for the fuselage.[2]

In developing the stealthy SR-71, Lockheed apparently drew heavily on earlier government-supported research efforts. The U.S. Air Force Avionics Laboratory at Wright-Patterson Air Force Base, working closely with industry, supported much of the pioneering theoretical and applied research on reducing radar signature in the 1950s. Efforts to accurately measure aircraft RCS began early in that decade. As engineers developed better methods for measuring RCS, interest in reducing RCS increased. Engineers examined the echo character-istics of specific aircraft on a special measurement range built for the purpose. By the mid-1950s, engineers began to investigate which el-ements of an aircraft's shape and configuration contributed most to radar echo, and how the configuration could be changed to reduce that echo. In 1955, a major effort was launched to develop radar-absorbing material to apply to aircraft structures. By the end of the decade, a Lockheed T-33 had been coated entirely in RAM and tested extensively. Screens for air inlets and masking of exhaust pipes were developed on two Boeing B-47 test-bed aircraft. Early on, this re-search had demonstrated that aircraft shape and configuration were the most important contributors to radar echo, and that significant

---

[2]Lockheed and Convair competed for this top-secret project sponsored by the Central Intelligence Agency (CIA). Convair submitted designs for small aircraft launched from the B-58 that would utilize ceramics for low RCS and heat resistance. In addition to fuselage shaping, Lockheed's design incorporated radar-absorbing plastic materials on the leading-edge flaps and control surfaces, as well as ferrous coatings and other composite materials on the fuselage. While not known at the time by North American, the go-ahead for the Lockheed Blackbird contributed directly to the cancellation of its Mach-3 F-108 Rapier, as well as rejection of proposals to save the XB-70 program by modifying the bomber into a strategic reconnaissance aircraft. See Rich and Janos (1994, p. 24); Lynch (1992, p. 23); and Sweetman and Goodall (1990, pp. 13–14).

reduction in RCS required full application of RCS concepts to the basic aircraft design from the beginning of development. These results clearly influenced Lockheed's design approach to the SR-71.[3]

Lockheed's experience with developing low-RCS configurations and materials grew in the 1960s as the Skunk Works continued its specialization in covert reconnaissance aircraft. Basic research on materials, aerodynamics, and other areas continued at Lockheed's Rye Canyon laboratories in California. Early in the decade, Lockheed began development of a stealthy reconnaissance drone that was originally intended for launch from the SR-71. Called the D-21, the drone entered a flight-test program in 1966. Shaped like an SR-71 nacelle with blended wings attached, the small, unmanned stealth vehicle reportedly had very good performance: Weighing only 13,000 lb loaded, it reportedly had an intercontinental range and could attain speeds of nearly Mach 4 and altitudes of 100,000 ft (Rich and Janos, 1994, pp. 22–23; Sweetman and Goodall, 1990, p. 15).

Other companies worked on various aspects of stealth in the 1960s. Beginning in 1960, Ryan Aeronautical Company produced a wide variety of stealthy reconnaissance drones that included fuselage-shaping and RAM (Wagner, 1982). General Dynamics, the loser in the U-2 competition, built an extensive RCS range and tested its TFX designs there. The firm later built another major range for the Air Force. Apparently, Northrop began concentrating on stealth research in the mid-1960s and gained important experience on stealth during this period, although few details are publicly available. According to one account, Northrop's research focused on attaining very low RCS without compromising aerodynamic performance. By the early 1970s, the Defense Advanced Research Projects Agency (DARPA) was funding much of this research under a highly classified program called Harvey (Dorr, 1995, p. 11; Sweetman and Goodall, 1992, p. 18).

Not being able to maintain good aerodynamic capabilities and maneuverability had always been viewed as a problem in shaping airframes for stealth, and it may explain why so many years passed before contractors made serious attempts to develop very-low-RCS

---

[3]A fascinating account of early Air Force research on stealth can be found in Bahret (1993).

fighters and bombers. At one point, Lockheed officials considered offering a modification of the D-21 to the Air Force as a stealthy attack aircraft. But, as discussed in Chapter Five, fighter design in the 1960s was moving away from an emphasis on high speed and high altitude to enhanced maneuverability. Engineers in the 1960s believed that the fuselage shaping and added weight of RAM treatments to obtain low RCS would unacceptably degrade required aerodynamic qualities. To attain very low RCS, the aircraft might not even be controllable, given the flight-control technology of the 1960s. By the early 1970s, however, many of these problems appeared more amenable to solution. General Dynamics had developed a sophisticated analog FBW flight-control system for the YF-16. Progress was being made in RAM and in the development of lightweight carbon-fiber composite (CFC) materials for structural use.

THE F-117 COMPETITION

DARPA awarded competitive study contracts to Northrop, McDonnell-Douglas, and three other contractors in 1974 to develop design concepts for a very-low-RCS combat aircraft. DARPA intended to award the winner of the competition a contract to develop and fly two technology-demonstration prototypes. Lockheed also soon joined the competition.[4] Its engineers developed a highly unconventional faceted design nicknamed the "Hopeless Diamond," which contained only two-dimensional flat surfaces. The reason for this flat-surface design was that RCS could be calculated with high precision only for two-dimensional surfaces, given the state of knowledge and the capability of computers at the time. Northrop is thought to have proposed a more conventional delta-wing stealth design with the air inlet on top, which used a combination of angular and rounded surfaces (Sweetman and Goodall, 1992, p. 23). In October, DARPA selected the Northrop and Lockheed designs as the finalists. The two companies built models of their designs, and engineers tested the models in early 1976 on a fixed pole in a competitive

---

[4]Defense Department officials had not sent out the original RFP to Lockheed because they were unaware of the firm's pioneering stealth work on the highly classified SR-71 and D-21 programs conducted for the CIA. Each of the original five contractors received $1 million, but Lockheed had to finance its effort with corporate funds. See Rich and Janos (1994, pp. 22–25).

fly-off at the Air Force's radar range in New Mexico. In April, DARPA informed Lockheed that it had won the competition.

Under a program code-named Have Blue, jointly sponsored by the Air Force and DARPA, Lockheed received a new contract to build and flight-test two small manned technology demonstrators labeled XST (Experimental Survivable Testbed)[5] to demonstrate and validate its stealth technologies and design. Except for their shape and materials, these test vehicles were largely conventional, using mostly off-the-shelf components and subsystems, such as a modified version of the GD F-16 FBW flight-control system complete with its side-stick controller, and the landing gear from the Northrop F-5.

In 1976, the Air Force and various government agencies were supporting several contractor studies to examine operational applications of stealth technology to different mission areas and types of air vehicles. A government "Blue Team" was also looking at similar issues. These studies led to recommendations to the Air Force encouraging the development of low-RCS fighter, attack, and bomber aircraft, as well as cruise missiles and Unmanned Air Vehicles (UAVs). In response, the Air Force is said to have initiated the Covert Survivable In-weather Reconnaissance/Strike (CSIRS) program, which led to a decision to develop a stealthy tactical attack fighter and a tactical reconnaissance platform.

The Air Force moved ahead rapidly to support development of an operational stealth fighter/attack aircraft based on the XST. The resulting F-117 went on to complete development and become an effective fighter/attack aircraft tested in combat (Kennedy et al., 1992). In 1992, during Desert Storm in Iraq, the F-117 demonstrated the operational benefits of stealth when combined with precision-guided munitions and other assets.

THE ADVANCED TECHNOLOGY BOMBER COMPETITION

Northrop's loss to Lockheed for the XST did not end its pioneering efforts in stealth. The Air Force and DARPA awarded Northrop a

---

[5]Although open press sources usually claim that XST stands for "Experimental Stealth Technology Testbed," Dorr (1995, p. 11) insists that "Experimental Survivable Testbed" is actually correct.

sole-source contract in 1978, in part based on its strong performance on the XST competition, for development of a new stealthy technology demonstrator called Tacit Blue.[6] Initially, Tacit Blue was part of the Pave Mover program aimed at developing a stealthy reconnaissance aircraft with an LPI radar for operation very close to the forward battle lines. Reportedly, the Air Force soon concluded that the battlefield ground-surveillance mission could be conducted by a larger, more conventional aircraft flying much farther behind the front lines. This conclusion led to the Grumman E-8 Joint Surveillance Target Attack Radar System (JSTARS) surveillance aircraft based on the Boeing 707 airliner airframe. The Air Force decided to continue flight-testing the Tacit Blue demonstrator as a generic test bed for stealth technologies.

In 1978, Lockheed won a 2-year concept formulation contract to study the development of a stealthy medium tactical bomber in the F-111 class, which could be based on a scaled-up version of the F-117. Over time, the Lockheed design evolved toward a flying-wing concept, because such an approach provided low RCS and good wing efficiency for long range and a large payload. Later, Northrop also began proposing bomber designs and received its own design study contracts. Through the Tacit Blue program, Northrop already had experience designing low-observable aircraft with rounded shapes. It may also have drawn on the experience from other technology demonstrators that were allegedly under development at the time. Eventually, Northrop developed its N-14 design, a flying wing (Rich and Janos, 1994, pp. 302–307; Baker, 1994a, p. 144).

The Advanced Technology Bomber (ATB) program soon evolved into a very-high-stakes competition between the two emerging leaders in stealth technology: Lockheed and Northrop. In early 1981, at Defense Department urging, the two contractors sought out team partners in order to provide more resources to support such a potentially large program. Lockheed teamed with Rockwell; Northrop teamed with Boeing and LTV. These were ideal teams from the perspective of experience. Lockheed, of course, was the pioneer developer of the first stealth fighter, and Rockwell, with its XB-70, B-1A, and B-1B, was the leading bomber developer of the past two decades.

---

[6]This account is drawn from Lopez (1996, p. 17).

Northrop benefited from Boeing's long experience with bombers and its vast knowledge of large-aircraft development. Its lack of experience in supersonic fighter and bomber development was, of course, irrelevant: The stealth bomber would be subsonic. In addition, both Boeing and LTV were industry leaders in composite-materials design and manufacture, particularly in large load-bearing structures.

As with the XST several years earlier, the Air Force organized a "shoot-out" between the two competing designs in May 1981 at a radar range to determine which had the lower RCS. The Air Force also conducted wind-tunnel tests to calculate lift-to-drag ratios so that potential range could be determined. In October, the Air Force formally awarded the ATB development contract to Northrop. Ben Rich of Lockheed claims that his company's design tested out with a lower RCS. However, the Lockheed proposal called for a considerably smaller aircraft than the Northrop submission, and it had inferior range and payload capabilities (Rich and Janos, 1994, pp. 309–311).

Northrop's earlier innovative and pioneering activities in directly related design and technology areas may have been the key to its victory in the competition. As one published account notes, developing the ATB entailed significant technological risks relating to the aircraft's "complex curvatures, exotic materials, and other stealth methods" (Scott, 1991a, pp. 7–8). In 1981, Northrop was developing Tacit Blue and may have already been flying a prototype LO reconnaissance vehicle for many months at the time it won the ATB competition. Northrop would have accumulated more experience than Lockheed in designing and developing the large curved and rounded stealth designs necessary for long-range heavy bombers with Have Blue and other programs that might have existed.[7]

---

[7]Available sources claim that Northrop's flying wings from the late 1940s—the XB-35 and YB-49—provided little data and few insights relevant to the ATB development effort: Most engineers involved with the earlier efforts had long since retired, and Northrop had great difficulty locating test data that had been recorded during the earlier programs. However, engineers and test pilots did consult extensively with pilots who had flown the YB-49. See Scott (1991a, pp. 9, 60).

THE ADVANCED TACTICAL FIGHTER COMPETITION

By far the richest and most sought-after prize of the stealth era remained the development contract for the first Air Force supersonic stealth fighter to replace the F-15 air-superiority fighter. As effective as it was, the F-117 remained a subsonic attack aircraft used primarily for air-to-ground operations. The leading prime contractors soon realized how important the competition for the next Air Force air-superiority fighter would be. In all likelihood, it would be the only opportunity to develop a new first-line fighter for the next decade or more.

Because of anticipated high R&D costs and multiple competing demands on the defense budget, the Defense Department envisioned at most only one major new fighter-development program and one major attack-aircraft effort for the 1980s and 1990s: the Advanced Tactical Fighter (ATF) and the Advanced Tactical Aircraft (ATA). At least eight remaining U.S. prime contractors competed strenuously for these two development efforts: General Dynamics, McDonnell-Douglas, Lockheed, Northrop, Boeing, Grumman, North American–Rockwell, and LTV. It was believed at the time that at least some of the losers would ultimately have to withdraw as prime contractors from the fighter/attack aircraft market.

The U.S. Air Force launched the ATF program in June 1981 with a Request for Information (RFI) to U.S. prime contractors. At that time, the U.S. Navy was examining the possibility of seeking a new common fighter (labeled the VMFX) to replace both the Grumman F-14 fighter and the Grumman A-6 attack aircraft.[8] However, in 1983, the Navy dropped this approach as too expensive and replaced it with a new plan to upgrade existing F-14s and A-6s and to procure a new stealthy attack aircraft, called the Advanced Tactical Aircraft. Thus, after 1983, U.S. contractors could expect at most only one major development program for a new air-superiority fighter and one other program for an attack aircraft over at least the next decade.

In September 1985, the Air Force sent out RFPs for a demonstration and validation (Dem/Val) phase for the ATF. Seven prime contrac-

---

[8]Boeing won a contract for a major upgrade program for the A-6. The radically changed A-6F included a new, all-composite wing designed and developed by Boeing.

tors responded with serious design proposals. DoD and the U.S. Air Force selected Lockheed and Northrop in October 1986 to lead competing teams during a planned 54-month Dem/Val phase of the ATF development program. Only one team, of course, would receive the final award for full-scale development at the end of the competitive Dem/Val stage. In 1986, the Navy also awarded competitive design contracts for the ATA to two teams: one led by Northrop, which included Grumman and LTV, and one with McDonnell-Douglas and General Dynamics as equal partners.

The outcome of the ATF competition surprised some observers. According to at least one open source, McDonnell-Douglas and General Dynamics had been considered the leading contenders in the very early phases of the program because of their past experience and clear leadership in conventional fighter development. But Lockheed and Northrop, it is claimed, because of their far more extensive knowledge and experience with stealth technologies, eventually submitted ATF design proposals that were considered more innovative and clearly superior to those of the other contractors in the area of stealth (Sweetman and Goodall, 1991b, p. 36). According to another published account, the Air Force rejected the McDonnell-Douglas design as insufficiently stealthy and too conservative; Boeing was rejected, in part, because of its lack of recent fighter-development experience (Sweetman and Goodall, 1991a, p. 34).[9] In addition, the overall approach adopted by the two winning contractors to fuselage shaping for lowering radar cross section seems to have emerged from each company's own unique past experience. The more-angular Lockheed design, designated the YF-22, in some respects is reminiscent of the F-117 with its faceted-flat-surface Hopeless Diamond approach. The competing YF-23 seems to have drawn on an approach similar to Northrop's XST, Tacit Blue, and B-2 designs by using a more rounded shape with only two continuous surfaces.

The Air Force encouraged the competing prime contractors to team up in groups to share both the financial risk and the experience base

---

[9]However, as in the case of past design proposals from the Seattle company dating back to the TFX/F-111, Boeing's ATF design proposal reportedly fared quite well on its own merits, allegedly coming in fourth in the competition (Sweetman and Goodall, 1991b, p. 37).

for the ATF, the only new first-line fighter program expected for decades. The two groups chosen as finalists were in many respects "dream teams." The Lockheed team combined the Skunk Work's unquestioned leadership in stealth technology built up with the XST and F-117 efforts, with General Dynamics' skills in fighter development based on the F-16 and F-111, and Boeing's extensive experience in composite materials and structures from commercial programs, the A-6F and the B-2 efforts. The second ATF team drew on Northrop's experience in stealth technology dating back to the XST and B-2 programs, as well as its skills in fighter development based on the YF-17/F-18 and the F-5 series.[10] Northrop teamed with McDonnell-Douglas, the leading U.S. fighter developer of the 1960s and 1970s.

For the ATA, Northrop again provided stealth and fighter R&D expertise; its team members Grumman and LTV shared their long experience with developing naval fighter and attack aircraft. The McDonnell-Douglas/General Dynamics team appeared unmatched in conventional fighter development experience; however, it seemed less strong in stealth aircraft R&D, particularly in GD's case. Both teams won follow-on contracts in June 1986 to refine their design proposals in anticipation of selection of one of the teams to lead full-scale development. Northrop's team proposal envisioned a larger and heavier aircraft than its competitor, with a projected development cost that was $1.1 billion higher than the design submitted by the McDonnell-Douglas/GD team (U.S. House of Representatives, 1992a, p. 186). In January 1988, the Navy selected the McDonnell-Douglas/GD team primarily on cost grounds. Unfortunately, by mid-1990, the A-12 program was at least $1 billion over cost and 18 months behind schedule. In January of the next year, Secretary of Defense Dick Cheney cancelled the program.[11]

---

[10]In the 1970s, Northrop developed a much-improved export fighter derived from the F-5E. Originally called the F-5G, this fighter was later designated the F-20 Tigershark. Although highly capable, the F-20 was never purchased by a foreign government, in part because the U.S. government began supporting foreign sales of first-line USAF fighters such as the F-16. Northrop eventually terminated the F-20 program.

[11]For a full account of the ill-fated A-12 program, see James Perry Stevenson, *The $5 Billion Misunderstanding: The Collapse of the Navy's Stealth Bomber Program*, Annapolis, Md.: Naval Institute Press, 2001.

In April 1991, after more than four years of development work and an extensive flight-test program, the Air Force selected the Lockheed/General Dynamics/Boeing YF-22 for full-scale development as the next Air Force air-superiority fighter. Reportedly, the Air Force considered both prototypes to be outstanding, but believed the YF-22 was a more balanced design and preferred the Lockheed industrial team (Sweetman and Goodall, 1991a, p. 40).[12] As of this writing, the F-22 program has nearly completed a largely successful full-scale development program, and it is likely to enter into low-rate production.[13]

INDUSTRY STRUCTURE DURING THE STEALTH REVOLUTION

The stunning innovation and technological breakthroughs witnessed during the stealth revolution took place in an environment of intense competition among as many as nine prime contractors. This highly competitive environment surely contributed to the successful outcomes of most programs. More important, Lockheed and Northrop—two extremely "hungry" second-rank fighter prime contractors that had been largely cut out of the conventional fighter market—pursued radical and innovative technologies in an attempt to dethrone the reigning leaders of the fighter market in the prestealth era: McDonnell-Douglas and General Dynamics.

In 1979, on the eve of the stealth technology revolution, at least five and as many as eight or nine large prime contractors could be viewed as potentially serious competitors for military combat aircraft R&D contracts. Six of these firms, whose total sales are shown in Figure 6.2, ranked among the top-100 firms by total sales in the United States. Note that Northrop and Lockheed were among the smallest in total sales among these firms. As lower-ranked firms had done in the past, they adopted a strategy of high-risk innovation in design

---

[12]Allegedly, the YF-23 was faster and stealthier, but the YF-22 was more maneuverable.

[13]The high unit cost and the changed threat environment have made the F-22 a controversial program. As of this writing, the decision to enter production and the ultimate numbers to be procured remain in doubt. Few doubt the performance virtuosity of the F-22.

and technology to try to knock the industry leaders out of their dominant positions.

By 1990, Northrop and Lockheed had arguably become the industry leaders in fighter and bomber aircraft because of the combination of their extensive firm-specific expertise in stealth technologies and their unparalleled system-specific experience developing stealthy

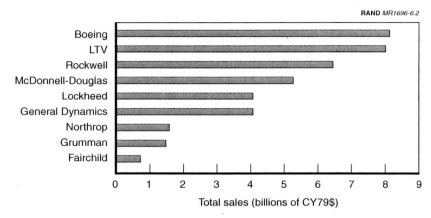

SOURCE: Data are from Donald M. Pattillo, *Pushing the Envelope: The American Aircraft Industry*, Ann Arbor, Michigan: The University of Michigan Press, 2000.
NOTE: Includes commercial and non-aerospace sales.

Figure 6.2—Leading Combat-Aircraft Contractors, 1979

bombers and fighters. McDonnell-Douglas and General Dynamics can be considered to have slipped back somewhat from their leading positions in fighter development established during the previous period, largely because they lacked firm-specific expertise in the early part of the period in certain technologies critical for stealth. Nevertheless, these two firms remained formidable competitors, enabled by their long history of fighter leadership; their development of such aircraft as the significantly upgraded F/A-18E/F, which included improved RCS characteristics; and their involvement in the YF-22, YF-23, and A-12 programs.

These four contractors, leaders in fighter R&D, exhibited the same key characteristic of the leaders of earlier periods: They carried out an almost-continuous stream of fighter R&D beginning in 1975. Boeing played a major role on the F-22 program and continued to compete vigorously for major military-aircraft contracts. However, all other prime contractors essentially exited from the fighter R&D business or were purchased by leading contractors.

A wrenching consolidation and downsizing of the U.S. aerospace in-dustry began in the early 1990s after the collapse of the Berlin Wall and with the end of the Cold War. In early 1993, Lockheed purchased General Dynamics' Fort Worth fighter division, ending nearly half a century of independent combat aircraft R&D leadership dating back to Consolidated's B-24 Liberator and the Convair delta jets of the 1940s and 1950s. In mid-1994, Lockheed and Martin-Marietta agreed to merge, adopting the new name of Lockheed-Martin. In April 1994, Northrop purchased Grumman, ending the independent existence of the company that had been the Navy's premier fighter developer since the mid-1930s. At the same time, Northrop completed its purchase of LTV.[14] In 1996, Boeing bought Rockwell's aerospace and defense divisions, the core of what had been North American–Rockwell, the developer of the most famous U.S. prop and subsonic fighters, as well as the first operational supersonic fighter. Boeing followed this move almost immediately by announcing an even bigger move, a merger with its long-time rival, McDonnell-Douglas. Finally, in July 1997 Northrop-Grumman agreed to be ac-quired by Lockheed-Martin.[15]

Thus, in just over four years, five historical leaders in fighter R&D ap-peared to have been eliminated as independent entities: General Dynamics, Grumman, McDonnell-Douglas, Northrop, and Rockwell. The number of prime contractors with credible capabilities to de-velop new combat aircraft had been reduced from eight to just two: Lockheed-Martin and Boeing.

SUMMARY

In the 1930s and 1940s, Germany and Great Britain pioneered the opening phases of the turbo-jet revolution. But the U.S. aerospace industry almost single-handedly carried out an equally dramatic technological revolution in the 1970s and 1980s: stealth. In 1997, the remaining two leading U.S. prime contractors in military aircraft R&D had attained a level of capability and experience in fighter and bomber development that far surpassed the level possessed by any

---

[14]Northrop had purchased a 49-percent interest in LTV in 1992.

[15]This proposed merger was eventually blocked as a result of growing anti-competition concerns at the Departments of Defense and Justice.

other national aerospace industry in the world. Yet the U.S. industry also confronted the prospect of even fewer new R&D programs to maintain its experience base. The proposed Lockheed-Northrop merger, although eventually blocked, had ignited serious concerns among policymakers about the future of competition and innovation in the U.S. fixed-wing combat-aircraft industrial base. From the historical record we have surveyed, are these concerns justified?

Chapter Seven

AN END TO COMPETITION AND INNOVATION?

The wrenching consolidation and downsizing of the U.S. aerospace industry that began in the early 1990s after the collapse of the Berlin Wall and with the end of the Cold War had, by the end of the 1990s, reduced from seven or eight to just two the number of prime contractors with credible capabilities to develop new combat aircraft: Lockheed-Martin and Boeing.[1]

Although the pace of first-tier consolidation slowed after the government blocked the Lockheed-Martin/Northrop Grumman proposed merger deal, concerns persisted about the reduced levels of competition in the industry and its effects on innovation and price. Uneasiness over declining competitiveness and a potential loss of innovation emerged from perceptions that, over the long term, insufficient numbers of fixed-wing combat aircraft and related technology projects would be available to support more than one or two full-design, Research, Development, Test and Evaluation (RDT&E),

---

[1]Northrop Grumman's future status remains uncertain. The company has already expanded well beyond its status as a defense electronics and information technology (IT) specialty house, and it is once again a platform/system integrator. In mid-1999, it acquired Ryan Aeronautical, thus inheriting the Global Hawk program for the development of a HALE UAV. In 2000, the firm acquired Litton Industries, along with its Ingalls Shipyard, one of the two remaining builders of Navy combat ships. In July 2002, Northrop Grumman announced the planned purchase of TRW, a leading developer and producer of military satellites and other aerospace products. Approval of this purchase made the Los Angeles–based company the second-largest U.S. defense contractor behind Lockheed-Martin. In addition, Northrop Grumman's 20-percent share of the Joint Strike Fighter program led by Lockheed-Martin may permit it to retain credible capabilities to lead the design and development of future combat aircraft.

and manufacturing engineering teams. This perception was particularly true for fighter aircraft projects, where it was widely believed that the Joint Strike Fighter (JSF) would be the last U.S. manned fighter development and procurement project for decades. With the selection of Lockheed-Martin in October 2001 to develop and produce JSF on a winner-take-all basis, concerns about future competition and innovation increased.

JSF: THE LAST FIGHTER COMPETITION?

The Department of Defense officially launched the Joint Advanced Strike Technology (JAST) program (the predecessor to the JSF program) in December 1994 by awarding Concept Definition and Design Research contracts to four contractors: Boeing, Lockheed-Martin, McDonnell-Douglas, and Northrop Grumman. Soon thereafter, McDonnell-Douglas, Northrop Grumman, and British Aerospace joined together as a single team in the competition. Intense competition continued among these contractor teams—all leading combat aircraft developers—for nearly two years. In November 1996, DoD selected Boeing and Lockheed-Martin as the winners to continue on into the Concept Demonstration Phase. Since the JSF was intended to fill the tactical combat aircraft–modernization needs for the Air Force, Navy, and Marine Corps, no other fighter programs appeared likely for decades to come. McDonnell-Douglas' elimination from the program led directly to the acquisition of the company by Boeing. Almost overnight, one of the preeminent U.S. fighter developers, and the dominant leader in this specialization from the 1960s through the 1980s, disappeared as an independent entity and became a division of the giant Boeing Company. After the downselect, Northrop Grumman and British Aerospace (later BAE Systems after acquisition of GEC Marconi), teamed with Lockheed-Martin to continue on the JSF program.

For five years during the Concept Development and Risk Reduction Phase (CDRR), Lockheed-Martin and Boeing engaged in a fierce competition for victory on the JSF. Both contractors considered this effort to be a must-win competition, fearing that the loser would be forced to exit the combat aircraft industry. This intense competition climaxed in the development of two highly innovative demonstrator aircraft, the Lockheed-Martin X-35 and the Boeing X-32, which engaged in parallel flight demonstrations. On 26 October 2001, the government announced the selection of Lockheed-Martin, teamed with Northrop Grumman and BAE Systems, to develop the JSF F-35 fighter. Following the downselect to one prime, many observers expressed considerable concern that Boeing would be forced to effectively withdraw from the fighter market sector, leaving only one viable fighter developer/integrator in the United States with a *de facto* monopoly on the market.

Indeed, for the first time since the emergence of an indigenous U.S. combat aircraft industrial base shortly following World War I, only one prime contractor will be involved in designing and developing a new fighter/attack aircraft that will meet the manned fighter aircraft needs of all three services for decades.[2] On the surface, this situation appears far less conducive to future competition than even the situation in the 1920s, when only two contractors dominated the fighter market and two dominated the bomber market.

It has been argued in this report that the biplane era during the 1920s was a period of relative design and technological stagnation, and that these characteristics were in part due to the small number of credible combat aircraft developers and the relative lack of competition. However, a common thread that runs through all the periods of revolutionary innovation in our historical analysis, dating back to the monoplane revolution, is that the key innovating firms were almost always second-rank prime contractors, companies either moving into new areas of aircraft specialization or totally new entrants. The question that concerns many analysts now is: With only one remaining dominant developer of advanced U.S. fighter aircraft, and with almost insurmountable barriers to new entrants from outside the industry, what companies in the future will play the role of the second-rank firms in the past? What companies will take the great risks of radical innovation to beat the industry leader in the next competition? Will Boeing or perhaps even Northrop Grumman, with its large share of the JSF program, be able to play that role?

Certainly much has changed since the era of the biplane. Not least important, the U.S. government appears to be returning to

---

[2]Boeing is developing an Unmanned Combat Air Vehicle (UCAV), and Northrop Grumman has several UAV programs under way.

historically high levels of R&D and procurement. A key cause of the stagnation in the 1920s was the lack of demand. Also important, the JSF prime contractor anticipates a huge domestic market supplemented by potentially large foreign markets. Extensive sales overseas will come only after intense competition with highly capable foreign prime contractors offering their own advanced fighter designs. In addition, Boeing, Northrop Grumman, and other U.S. contractors will likely win major contracts to develop and integrate UAVs and UCAVs and other systems, all sophisticated air vehicles that may require similar skills to fighter development and that may compete directly or indirectly with the JSF, both in domestic and foreign markets. Northrop Grumman may also retain considerable fighter design, development, and production experience through its participation in the JSF program.

Whether future decades will more closely resemble the technologically stagnant biplane era of the 1920s or periods of revolutionary innovation such as the 1930s, 1950s, and other more-recent periods remains to be seen.

Our high-level survey of the history of innovation in the U.S. combat aircraft industry raises serious questions about the future of the industry. Unfortunately, the historical evidence we surveyed does not conclusively demonstrate the precise linkages between industry structure, competition, and innovation. Clearly, other key factors, such as government R&D and spending policies, the level of government demand, government procurement policies, operational military requirements, a wide variety of issues related to the states of technology development and the posture of the broader economy, can play crucial roles in spurring new periods of high innovation in combat aircraft.

CONCLUSIONS

Our broad assessment of the industry dynamics during each of the historical technology eras described earlier in this report has thus produced a variety of observations and hypotheses, most of which require further testing and analysis. The validity of these observations and hypotheses and how they apply to the current and future conditions that may characterize the U.S. combat aircraft industrial base require further research. Nonetheless, they are worth repeating at least as a guide for further research.[3] They include the following:

- Each of the five historical technology eras we identified began with distinct periods characterized by bursts of dramatically increased innovation in combat aircraft. The resulting new combat aircraft based on new designs and technology exhibited significant advances in performance capabilities over the previous generation of combat aircraft.

- The initial periods of high technological innovation that began each technology era were all characterized by an increased competition to innovate among at least seven experienced, credible prime contractors/integrators.

- Following the initial period of increased innovation that started each new technology era, prime contractors tended to focus on refinement of the new technologies and configuration that had recently emerged. Except for the period of biplane technology consolidation in the 1920s, these periods were also characterized by vigorous competition among at least seven credible prime contractors. Contractors continued to innovate, except at a pace that was slower, less revolutionary. Eventually, however, the designs and technologies characteristic of the specific technology era reached a point of dramatically diminishing marginal returns in engine/platform performance.

- After an initial industry shake-out following the period of high technology innovation in each new technology era, new dominant industry leaders among prime contractors/integrators emerged in key specialty areas in combat aircraft. Other companies declined to positions that could be characterized as second-rank or niche players in terms of reputation, winning program competitions, and/or sector sales.

- From the historical evidence, the precise relationship between competition and increased innovation at the beginning of each new technology era is unclear. The competition to innovate during these periods was usually triggered by factors related to

---

[3]RAND has conducted a larger parallel study of projected future conditions and structure of the defense aerospace industry to test these and other hypotheses (Birkler et al., 2003).

increased market demand, various technology developments, and military threat perceptions and system requirements.

More specifically, the types of factors that historically seem to be linked to high-innovation bursts and the increased competition to innovate that began each new technology era include (1) industry perceptions of a potential or actual increase in market demand, (2) maturity and applicability of new component technologies, particularly when a new design and technology approach promised to offer high returns in desirable performance improvements, and/or (3) significant changes in government buyer performance and capability requirements.

- The prime contractors that tended to be the technology leaders and greatest innovators during the periods with initial bursts of intense competition to innovate that began each new technology era, were most often not among the industry leaders of the prior technology-refinement era. Rather, they were one of the following types of firms:

  — Second-rank or niche prime contractors

  — Leader firms expanding outside their existing area of specialization

  — New entrants to the industry.

- The historical evidence suggests, but does not prove, that an industrial structure that includes numerous prime contractors during periods of slower technological advance, some of which are dominant in sales and some of which are second-rank, is conducive to encouraging the onset of periods of higher innovation when demand changes and market conditions are right. To displace the dominant market leaders, second-rank firms are willing to take greater technological and financial risks, thus setting off an intense competition to innovate among many qualified contractors seeking market expansion.

- Our more detailed review of the 1920s and the early 1930s seems to support, but does not prove, the contention that larger numbers of experienced, credible prime contractors are more likely than lower numbers of competitors to promote the greater competition to innovate that leads to new technology eras. Unlike any other historical period, the post–World War I biplane era was dominated by only two credible and experienced developers of fighters and one or two leading developers of bombers. U.S. innovation in military aircraft slowed dramatically, to the point of stagnation during this period. This period was characterized by both the smallest number of dominant prime contractors in fixed-wing military aircraft and arguably the lowest level of sustained technological innovation of any comparable period in U.S. aviation history. However, the relative lack of innovation during this period was also strongly influenced by the low demand and lack of market opportunities. Furthermore, the existence of relatively low entry barriers meant that, when demand increased, competition and innovation went up.

- The historical evidence suggests, but does not prove, that higher levels of demand promote new entrants and much greater competition among contractors to innovate. The existence of only one or two dominant credible contractors, combined with high barriers to entry, may reduce the incentives for competition to innovate, even during periods of rising demand.

We find that these conclusions raise potentially serious questions about the level of competition and innovation in a future environment that may be dominated by only one or two prime contractors with the credible capability to develop a new-generation fixed-wing combat aircraft. These questions require further study and analysis.

Anderson, Fred, *Northrop: An Aeronautical History*, Hawthorne, Calif.: Northrop Corporation, 1976.

Anderton, David A., *Republic F-105 Thunderchief*, London: Osprey Publishing Ltd., 1983.

___, *North American Super Sabre*, London: Osprey Publishing Ltd., 1987.

Armitage, Michael, *Unmanned Aircraft*, London: Brassey's Defense Publishers, 1988.

Art, Robert J., *The TFX Decision: McNamara and the Military*, Boston, Mass.: Little, Brown & Company, 1968.

Auburn University Library, Rickenbacker Papers, Eddie Rickenbacker page. URL: http://www.lib.auburn.edu/archive/flyhy/101/eddie.htm#ww1 (5 March 2003).

Bahret, William F., "The Beginnings of Stealth Technology," *IEEE Transactions on Aerospace and Electronic Systems*, October 1993.

Baker, David, "Wizard Wars & Air Power in the 21st Century," *Air International*, September 1994a.

___, "From ATF to Lightning II: A Bolt in Anger," *Air International*, December 1994b.

Bavousett, Glenn B., *Combat Aircraft of World War II*, New York: Bonanza, 1989.

Biddle, Wayne, *Barons of the Sky*, New York: Simon & Schuster, 1991.

Biery, Frederick, *International Collaboration in the Commercial Aircraft Industry*, Santa Monica, Calif.: RAND, unpublished manuscript, October 1978.

___, *Why Do We Buy the Weapons We Do? A Review of One Explanation*, Santa Monica, Calif.: RAND, unpublished manuscript, April 1980.

Bilstein, Roger E., *The Enterprise of Flight: The American Aviation and Aerospace Industry*, Washington and London: The Smithsonian Institution Press, 2001.

Birkler, John, Anthony G. Brower, Jeffrey A. Drezner, Gordon Lee, Mark Lorell, Giles Smith, Fred Timson, William P. G. Trimble, and Obaid Younossi, *Competition and Innovation in the U.S. Fixed-Wing Military Aircraft Industry*, Santa Monica, Calif.:   RAND, MR-1656-OSD, 2003.

Birkler, John, John C. Graser, Mark V. Arena, Cynthia R. Cook, Gordon Lee, Mark Lorell, Giles Smith, Fred Timson, Obaid Younossi, and Jon G. Grossman, *Assessing Competitive Strategies for the Joint Strike Fighter: Opportunities and Options*, Santa Monica, Calif.: RAND, MR-1362-OSD/JSF, 2001.

Boatman, John, "USA Planned Stealthy UAV to Replace SR-71," *Jane's Defence Weekly*, 17 December 1994.

Bodilly, Susan J., *Case Study of Risk Management in the USAF B-1B Bomber Program*, Santa Monica, Calif.: RAND, N-3616-AF, 1993.

Bowers, Peter M., *Boeing Aircraft Since 1916*, Annapolis, Md.: Naval Institute Press, 1989.

Braybrook, Roy, "F-14 and F-15: The New Wave of Warplanes," *Air Enthusiast*, March 1972.

Bright, Charles D., *The Jet Makers: The Aerospace Industry from 1945 to 1972*, Lawrence, Kansas: The Regents Press of Kansas, 1978.

Burton, James, *The Pentagon Wars: Reformers Challenge the Old Guard*, Annapolis, Md.: Naval Institute Press, 1993.

Coulam, Robert F., *Illusions of Choice: The F-111 and the Problems of Weapons Acquisition Reform*, New York: Princeton University Press, 1977.

Delusach, Al, "Long Preparation Paid Off for McDonnell on the F-15," *St. Louis Post-Dispatch*, 11–12 January 1970.

Donald, David, ed., *The Complete Encyclopedia of World Aircraft*, New York: Barnes & Noble Books, 1999.

Dorr, Robert F., *Lockheed F-117 Nighthawk*, London: Aerospace Publishing Ltd., 1995.

Drezner, Jeffrey A., Giles K. Smith, Lucille E. Horgan, Curt Rogers, and Rachel Schmidt, *Maintaining Future Military Aircraft Capability*, Santa Monica, Calif.: RAND, R-4199-AF, 1992.

Ethell, Jeff, *F-15 Eagle*, London: Ian Allan Ltd., 1981.

Ford, Daniel, "The Worst Fighter of World War II? The Sorry Saga of the Brewster Buffalo," *Air & Space Smithsonian*, June/July 1996.

Francillon, René, *McDonnell Douglas Aircraft Since 1920: Volume I*, 2nd ed., rev. and updated, Annapolis, Md.: Naval Institute Press, 1990a.

___, *McDonnell Douglas Aircraft Since 1920: Volume II*, 2nd ed., rev. and updated, Annapolis, Md.: Naval Institute Press, 1990b.

___, *McDonnell Douglas F-15A/B*, Arlington, Texas: Aerofax, Inc., 1984.

Gentry, Jerauld R., *Evolution of the F-16 Multinational Fighter*, Student Research Report, Washington, D.C.: Industrial College of the Armed Forces, 1976.

Gething, Michael J., *F-15*, New York: Arco Publishing Inc., 1983.

Glenn L. Martin Aviation Museum, *Martin Aircraft Specifications*, Middle River, Md., 1998.

Godfrey, David W. H., "B-1 Airborne Strategic Deterrent," *Air International*, February 1975.

___, "B-1 Design Has Forward Fins," *Aviation Week & Space Technology*," 4 May 1970.

___, "Dogfighter Supreme: The Tomcat," *Air Enthusiast International*, January 1977a.

___, "Hawkeye: A New Dimension in Tactical Warfare," *Air Enthusiast International*, January 1977b.

Goodwin, Jacob, *Brotherhood of Arms: General Dynamics and the Business of Defending America*, New York: Times Books, 1985.

Green, William, and Gordon Swanborough, *The Complete Book of Fighters*, New York: Smithmark, 1994.

Guenther, Ben, and Jay Miller, *Bell X-1 Variants*, Arlington, Texas: Aerofax, 1988.

Gunston, Bill, *Attack Aircraft of the West*, New York: Charles Scribner's Sons, 1974.

___, *Combat Aircraft*, New York: Chartwell, 1978a.

___, *The Encyclopedia of the World's Combat Aircraft*, New York: Chartwell, 1978b.

___, *The Encyclopedia of World Air Power*, New York: Crescent Books, 1980.

___, *F-111*, New York: Arco Publishing Inc., 1983.

___, *F/A-18 Hornet*, London: Ian Allen Ltd., 1985.

___, *Jet Bombers from the Messerschmitt Me 262 to the Stealth B-2*, London: Osprey Publishing Ltd., 1993.

___, *Modern Airborne Missiles*, London: Arco Publishing Inc., 1983.

___, *Modern Fighting Aircraft*, New York: The Military Press, 1984.

Hall, G. R., and R. E. Johnson, *Transfers of United States Aerospace Technology to Japan*, Santa Monica, Calif.: RAND, P-3875, July 1968.

Hallion, Richard P., "A Troubling Past: Air Force Fighter Acquisition Since 1945," *Air Power Journal*, Winter 1990, Vol. IV, No. 4, pp. 4–23.

Heppenheimer, T. A., *Turbulent Skies: The History of Commercial Aviation*, Sloan Technology Series, New York: John Wiley & Sons, 1995.

Holder, William G., *Boeing B-52 Stratofortress*, Fallbrook, Calif.: Aero Publishers Inc., 1975.

Ingells, Douglas, *L-1011 TriStar and the Lockheed Story*, Fallbrook, Calif.: Aero Publishers Inc., 1973.

Johnson, Clarence L., and Maggie Smith, *Kelly: More Than My Share of It All*, Washington, D.C.: Smithsonian Institution Press, 1985.

Johnson, L. L., *The Century Series Fighters: A Study in Research and Development*, Santa Monica, Calif.: RAND, May 1960 (not available for public release).

Jones, Lloyd S., *U.S. Bombers: 1928 to 1980s*, Fallbrook, Calif.: Aero Publishers, 1980.

___, *U.S. Fighters: Army–Air Force, 1920–1980s*, Fallbrook, Calif.: Aero Publishers, 1975.

___, *U.S. Naval Fighters*, Fallbrook, Calif.: Aero Publishers, 1977.

Kennedy, Dee, et al., "Dawn of Stealth," *Lockheed Horizons: We Own the Night*, May 1992.

Kennedy, Michael, Susan Resetar, and Nicole DeHoratius, *Holding the Lead: Sustaining a Viable U.S. Military Fixed-Wing Aeronautical R&D Industrial Base*, Santa Monica, Calif.: RAND, MR-777-AF, 1996.

Klein, Burton H., et al., *Research and Development Policies*, Santa Monica, Calif.: RAND, R-333, December 1958.

Knaack, Marcelle Size, *Post World War II Bombers: 1945–1973*, Washington, D.C.: Office of Air Force History, 1988.

___, *Post–World War II Fighters: 1945–1973*, Washington, D.C.: Office of Air Force History, 1978.

Kotz, Nick, *Wild Blue Yonder: Money, Politics and the B-1 Bomber*, New York: Pantheon Books, 1988.

Lewis, Kevin N., "Force Modernization and Recapitalization: A Few Lessons Suggested by History," Santa Monica, Calif.: unpublished RAND research.

Lopez, Ramon, "Out of the Black Comes Tacit Blue," *Flight International*, 8–14 May 1996.

Lorell, Mark A., "An Overview of Military Jet Engine History," Appendix B in Obaid Younossi, Mark V. Arena, Richard M. Moore, Mark A. Lorell, Joanna Mason, and John C. Graser, *Military Jet Engine Acquisition: Technology Basics and Cost-Estimating Methodology*, Santa Monica, Calif.: RAND, MR-1596-AF, 2002.

___, *Troubled Partnership: A History of U.S.–Japan Collaboration on the FS-X Fighter*, New Brunswick, N.J.: Transaction, 1996.

Lorell, Mark A., with Donna Kim Hoffman, *The Use of Prototypes in Selected Foreign Fighter Aircraft Development Programs: Rafale, EAP, Lavi, and Gripen*, Santa Monica, Calif.: RAND, R-3687-P&L, September 1989.

Lorell, Mark A., with Alison Sanders and Hugh Levaux, *Bomber R&D Since 1945: The Role of Experience*, Santa Monica, Calif.: RAND, MR-670-AF, December 1995.

Lorell, Mark A., and Hugh P. Levaux, *The Cutting Edge: A Half Century of U.S. Fighter Aircraft R&D*, Santa Monica, Calif.: RAND, MR-939-AF, 1998.

Lorell, Mark A., Julia Lowell, Michael Kennedy, and Hugh Levaux, *Cheaper, Faster, Better? Commercial Approaches to Weapons Acquisition*, Santa Monica, Calif.: RAND, MR-1147-AF, 2000.

Lynch, David J., "How the Skunk Works Fielded Stealth," *Air Force Magazine*, November 1992.

Martin, Tom, and Rachel Schmidt, *A Case Study of the F-20 Tigershark*, Santa Monica, Calif.: RAND, P-7495-RGS, June 1987.

Mason, Francis K., *Phantom: A Legend in Its Own Time*, Osceola, Wisc.: Motorbooks International, 1983.

Mayer, Kenneth R., *The Political Economy of Defense Contracting*, New Haven, Conn.: Yale University Press, 1991.

Mendenhall, Charles A., *Delta Wings: Convair's High-Speed Planes of the Fifties and Sixties*, Osceola, Wisc.: Motorbooks International, 1983.

Miller, Jay, *Convair B-58*, Arlington, Texas: Aerofax, Inc., 1985.

___, *General Dynamics F-16 Fighting Falcon*, Arlington, Texas: Aerofax, Inc., 1982.

___, *Lockheed SR-71 (A/12YF-12/D-21)*, Arlington, Texas: Aerofax, Inc., 1983a.

___, *The X-Planes: X-1 to X-29*, Marine on St. Croix, Minn.: Specialty Press, 1983b.

Mintz, John, "Navy Defers Repayment Demand on Stealth Plane; Move Seen as Reprieve for McDonnell Douglas," *The Washington Post*, 16 December 1992.

Munson, Kenneth, *Fighters Between the Wars, 1919–39*, London: Blandford Press, 1970a.

___, *Bombers Between the Wars, 1919–39*, New York: The MacMillan Company, 1970b.

Munson, Kenneth, and Gordon Swanborough, *Boeing: An Aircraft Album No. 4*, New York: Arco Publishing Inc., 1972.

Orr, Kelly, *Hornet: The Inside Story of the F/A-18*, Shrewsbury, England: Airlife Publishing, 1991.

Pace, Steve, *Edwards Air Force Base: Experimental Flight Test Center*, Osceola, Wisc.: Motorbooks International, 1994.

___, *Lockheed Skunk Works*, Osceola, Wisc.: Motorbooks International, 1992.

___, *Valkyrie: North American XB-70A*, Fallbrook, Calif.: Aero Publishers Inc., 1984.

Pattillo, Donald M., *Pushing the Envelope: The American Aircraft Industry*, Ann Arbor, Mich.: The University of Michigan Press, 2000.

Perry, Robert L., *The Antecedents of the X-1*, Santa Monica, Calif.: RAND, P-3154, June 1965.

___, *A Prototype Strategy for Aircraft Development*, Santa Monica, Calif.: RAND, July 1972 (not available for public release).

___, *Variable Sweep: A Case History of Multiple Re-Innovation*, Santa Monica, Calif.: RAND, P-3459, October 1966.

Pint, Ellen M., and Rachel Schmidt, *Financial Condition of U.S. Military Aircraft Prime Contractors*, Santa Monica, Calif.: RAND, MR-372-AF, 1994.

Prendergast, Curtis, *The First Aviators*, Alexandria, Va.: Time-Life Books, 1981.

Rich, Ben R., and Leo Janos, *Skunk Works: A Personal Memoir from the U-2 to the Stealth Fighter: The Inside Story of America's Most Secret Aerospace Company, the Airplanes They Built, and the Dangerous Missions That Won the Cold War*, Boston, Mass.: Little, Brown & Company, 1994.

Rich, Michael D., and Edward Dews, with C. L. Batten, *Improving the Military Acquisition Process: Lessons from RAND Research*, Santa Monica, Calif.: RAND, R-3373-AF/RC, 1986.

Scott, William B., *Inside the Stealth Bomber: The B-2 Story*, Blue Ridge Summit, Penn.: TAB/Aero Books, 1991a.

___, "TR-3A Evolved from Classified Prototypes Based on Tactical Penetrator Concept," *Aviation Week & Space Technology*, 10 June 1991b.

___, "Triangular Reconnaissance Aircraft May Be Supporting F-117A," *Aviation Week & Space Technology*, 10 June 1991c.

Scutts, J. C., *F-105 Thunderchief*, London: Ian Allen Ltd., 1981.

Serling, Robert J., *Legend and Legacy: The Story of Boeing and Its People*, New York: St. Martin's Press, 1992.

Shenon, Philip, "Jet Makers Preparing Bids for a Rich Pentagon Prize," *The New York Times*, 12 March 1996.

Smith, Giles K., A. A. Barbour, Thomas L. McNaugher, Michael D. Rich, and William L. Stanley, *The Use of Prototypes in Weapon System Development*, Santa Monica, Calif.: RAND, R-2345-AF, March 1981.

Smith, Giles K., and Ellen T. Friedmann, *An Analysis of Weapon System Acquisition Intervals, Past and Present*, Santa Monica, Calif.: RAND, R-2605-DR&E/AF, November 1980.

Sorrels, Charles A., *U.S. Missile Programs: Development, Deployment and Implications for Arms Control*, New York: McGraw-Hill Inc., 1983.

Sponsler, George C., N. Rubin, D. Gignoux, and E. Dare, *The F-4 and the F-14*, Gaithersburg, Md.: Columbia Research Corporation, May 1973.

Stevenson, James Perry, *The $5 Billion Misunderstanding: The Collapse of the Navy's Stealth Bomber Program*, Annapolis, Md.: Naval Institute Press, 2001.

___, *Grumman F-14 "Tomcat,"* Fallbrook, Calif.: Aero Publishers, 1975.

___, *McDonnell Douglas F-15 Eagle*, Fallbrook, Calif.: Aero Publishers, 1978.

___, *The Pentagon Paradox: The Development of the F-18 Hornet*, Annapolis, Md.: Naval Institute Press, 1993.

Stoff, Joshua, *The Thunder Factory: An Illustrated History of the Republic Aviation Corporation*, Osceola, Wisc.: Motorbooks International, 1990.

___, *Picture History of World War II American Aircraft Production*, New York: Dover, 1993.

Stuart, William G., *Northrop Case Study in Aircraft Design*, Hawthorne, Calif.: Northrop Corporation, September 1978.

Stubbing, Richard A., *The Defense Game*, New York: Harper & Row Publishers, 1986.

Swanborough, Gordon, *Military Transports and Training Aircraft of the World*, London: Temple Press Books, 1965.

___, *United States Military Aircraft Since 1909*, London & New York: Putnam, 1963.

___, *United States Navy Aircraft Since 1911*, London: Putnam, 1968.

Sweetman, Bill, *A-10 Thunderbolt II*, New York: Arco Publishing Inc., 1984a.

___, *Phantom*, London: Jane's Publishing Company Limited, 1984b.

___, *Stealth Bomber: Invisible Warplane, Black Budget*, Osceola, Wisc.: Motorbooks International, 1986.

Sweetman, Bill, and James Goodall, "The Fighter They Didn't Want," *World Airpower Journal*, Vol. 7, Autumn/Winter, 1991a.

___, *Lockheed F-117A: Operation and Development of the Stealth Fighter*, Osceola, Wisc.: Motorbooks International, 1990.

___, "Lockheed YF-22: Stealth with Agility," *World Airpower Journal*, Vol. 6, Summer 1991b.

___, *Northrop B-2 Stealth Bomber*, Osceola, Wisc.: Motorbooks International, 1992.

___, "Send in the Drones," *Popular Science*, October 1995.

Taylor, Michael J. H., *Boeing*, London: Jane's Publishing Company Limited, 1982.

___, ed., *Jane's Encyclopedia of Aviation*, New York: Crescent Books, 1995.

Thornborough, Anthony M., and Peter E. Davies, *Grumman A-6 Intruder Prowler*, London: Ian Allen Ltd., 1987.

U.S. House of Representatives, *The Navy's A-12 Aircraft Program*, Testimony Before the Procurement and Nuclear Systems Subcommittee, Research and Development Subcommittee, and

Investigations Subcommittee of the House Committee on the Armed Services, Washington, D.C.: USGPO, 1990.

___, *A-12 Acquisition*, Testimony Before the Investigation Subcommittee of the Committee on Armed Services, Washington, D.C.: USGPO, 1991a.

___, *A-12 Navy Aircraft*, Testimony Before the Legislation and National Security Subcommittee of the Committee on Government Operations, Washington, D.C.: USGPO, 1991b.

___, Committee on Armed Services, *A-12 Acquisition*, Washington, D.C.: USGPO, 1992a.

___, Committee on Government Operations, *Oversight Hearing on the A-12 Navy Aircraft*, Washington, D.C.: USGPO, 1992b.

Vander Meulen, Jacob A., *The Politics of Aircraft: Building an American Military Industry*, Lawrence, Kansas: University Press of Kansas, 1991.

Vartabedian, Ralph, "Pentagon Cancels Northrop Stealth Missile Program," *Los Angeles Times*, 10 December 1994, p. D1.

Wagner, William, *Lightning Bugs and Other Reconnaissance Drones*, Fallbrook, Calif.: Armed Forces Journal International and Aero Publishers Inc., 1982.

White, William D., *U.S. Tactical Air Power: Missions, Forces, and Costs*, Washington, D.C.: The Brookings Institution, 1974.

Yenne, Bill, *Lockheed*, New York: Crescent Books, 1980.

___, *McDonnell Douglas: A Tale of Two Giants*, New York: Crescent Books, 1985.

Yoshimura, Akira, *Zero Fighter*, Westport, Conn.: Praeger, 1996.

Younossi, Obaid, Mark V. Arena, Richard M. Moore, Mark A. Lorell, Joanna Mason, and John C. Graser, *Military Jet Engine Acquisition: Technology Basics and Cost-Estimating Methodology*, Santa Monica, Calif.: RAND, MR-1596-AF, 2002.